More praise for *Love Letters*

Love Letters is not only a reflection of Andris Baltins on the strength and goodness of his wife, Nancy, but a tribute to her and all mothers who care so passionately about their families and draw upon their inner wisdom and strength to guide and support their children with disabilities.

Paula Goldberg—*executive director, PACER Center, a parent advocacy organization in Minneapolis that trains parents to make a difference*

For those who wish to accord with the resonance of all life, Andris Baltins' *Love Letters* is a gift. With a heart and mind opened through intense encounters with impermanence—his own dire prognosis at age 37, and the death of his lifelong and beloved partner—Andris studies himself and the mysteries of life with inspiring honesty and uprightness. This intimacy is offered to us; one cannot help but be moved to receive it.

Tenshin Reb Anderson Roshi—*senior dharma teacher, San Francisco Zen Center*

Through these letters we also see that Andris and Nancy's teenaged son, who has Down syndrome, knows intuitively the importance of grieving the loss of his mother and demonstrates how to do so effectively. His remarkable insights and wisdom show us that unconditional love easily trumps intellectual disability.

Judy C. Martz—*former president,
National Down Syndrome Congress, Atlanta, GA*

Having recently lost my wife to ovarian cancer, I was apprehensive about reading another man's grief journey caused by the same disease. But I found reading *Love Letters* to be a warm and comforting glimpse of Andris Baltins' love, loss and grief relationship with his wife. This experience was so similar and yet so different from mine, but the similarities with another's experience are what I find most helpful.

John Zimmerman—*Lakeville, MN*

Love Letters

REFLECTIONS ON LIVING WITH LOSS

Andris A. Baltins

SYREN BOOK COMPANY

MINNEAPOLIS

Most Syren Books are available at special quantity discounts for bulk purchases for sales promotions, premiums, fund-raising, and educational needs. For details, write

Syren Book Company
Special Sales Department
5120 Cedar Lake Road
Minneapolis, MN 55416

Published by
Syren Book Company
5120 Cedar Lake Road
Minneapolis, MN 55416

Printed in Canada on acid-free paper

ISBN-13: 978-0-929636-70-2
ISBN-10: 0-929636-70-8

LCCN 2006934469

Cover design by Kyle G. Hunter
Book design by Ann Sudmeier

To order additional copies of this book see the form
at the back of this book or go to www.itascabooks.com

For my daughter and son,

in whom and with whom Nancy's presence
is forever manifest

FOREWORD

Stephen and Ondrea Levine

Twenty years ago, in *Who Dies?* I wrote that we speak of dying in wholeness, yet we see there are aspects of ourselves that have never fully seen the light of day. We see how much of ourselves is submerged, feels yet unborn, how much we push away life. It is as though we had never fully touched the ground of being. Never having placed our two feet squarely in the present, always shuffling and toe tapping, waiting for the next moment to arrive. I wrote that to become wholly born, whole beings, we must stop postponing life. To the degree that we postpone life, we postpone death. We deny death and life in one fell swoop.

Yet even authoring numerous texts and having over three decades of intimate experience with the dying does not fully prepare one for the immediacy of a terminal diagnosis of your beloved. Ondrea was recently diagnosed with leukemia. Twenty-six years of marriage, in which we have, I think, mirrored the ground of our being, are suddenly telescoped into a moment in time. The mirror is fractured.

This remarkable book brings clarity back to the mirror. This is a love story of a life well shared. It unveils for us the healing—albeit a healing unto death—of a woman who was an inspiration to all she touched. This is a book of rituals—rituals for opening the heart, rituals for finishing the unfinished business of life that continue the healing process well after the beloved has passed beyond. It is a recounting that personifies the truth that love never dies.

This book may well make you weep. Yet, paradoxically, it is in the heartfelt connection with pain that we find the joy of openness to our undying connection to the love we all share. That is the ground of our being.

Some might conclude that somehow, by continuing to live, Andris may have gotten the better of it. But, in truth, when we love someone fully, we might well wish he or she would die before us—so that we can offer that person the container for their dying process and stay behind to endure the rippings of grief. It is said that love is as close as we get to God—because to love fully, selflessly, with all our spiritual and physical energy, is God itself.

As Ondrea and I write this foreword, we grieve and we simultaneously celebrate the twenty-six years so far in our mutual healings into life and love. Life, love, and death all have a sorrow enfolded within them. That sorrow can be numbing. Or it can be fruitful. It is a fruitful sorrow that is projected from the pages of this book.

Ondrea and I embark on a road that is not fully illuminated. We will have to find our own way. Yet, we find comfort in knowing that Andris and Nancy have traveled a similar path before us, and we thank them for casting this beam of light—*Love Letters: Reflections on Living with Loss*—for our guidance.

Stephen and Ondrea Levine are internationally known speakers and writers on spirituality, relationships, and issues of death and dying. They have counseled terminally ill people and their families for more than thirty years and authored, together or individually, more than a dozen books, including *Who Dies? An Investigation of Conscious Living and Conscious Dying; Embracing the Beloved: Relationship as a Path of Awakening; Unattended Sorrow: Recovering from Loss and Reviving the Heart; and A Year to Live: How to Live This Year as if It Were Your Last.*

PREFACE

Henry A. Gustafson

This is a beautiful book. In thirty-nine letters written to Nancy, his deceased wife, Andris Baltins recounts his profound sense of loss experienced when confronting her dying and death. Although, in the midst of grief, the most ordinary tasks of daily living seemed overwhelming, in the letters it is clear that his immobilizing grief was relieved by gratitude. Memories of their shared experiences—of times of great happiness, of periods of life-threatening illnesses, of recognition of their growth and enrichment in parenting their two children: an academically talented daughter and a son born with Down syndrome—all have helped to relieve the sense of loss. Through recall, inventive creation of rituals and courage to do what seems helpful, the memories have become a sustaining resource for living into a hopeful future.

Perhaps most helpful to those of us who have yet to face the death of our life partner, we are allowed through these letters to observe how, for at least one thoughtful and reflective human being, memories that initially bring only a painful sense of loss are transformed through recall, inventive creation of rituals, and the courage to do what seems helpful instead of what seems conventional, into a sustaining resource for living into a hopeful future.

I had the privilege of meeting Nancy when she became a student at United Theological Seminary of the Twin Cities, where I was teaching New Testament Theology. To say that she was a remarkably creative and spiritually mature seminary student is an understatement. The depths of her explorations into the relationship of scripture to human faith and her perceptive applications of spiritual insight to human experience delighted those of us who helped her to discover the materials of the tradition. It goes without saying that Nancy—and, later Andy as well—became our teachers as well as our students. These two people enjoyed a rare relationship of spiritual intimacy that allowed curiosity, exploration, and differences of perspective to enhance their lives together rather than to threaten them. I am grateful for the ever-deepening friendship that continued with Nancy and Andy beyond her seminary years and allowed me to experience some of the astonishing richness of the ways in which they processed together the news of Nancy's cancer, and then the reality of its terminal nature, and, at last, the experience of her dying and death. Andy's account of his grief journey flows organically from what I observed of the relationship between the two of them, which came before, and has—in its sometimes startling honesty—the cohesion and integrity of an authentic human testimony.

The reader of these letters will recognize in them the influences of Jungian psychology, Christian teachings, Eastern religions, and contemporary philosophical writings—all of which provided the raw materials for the evolving worldview, and faithview, Nancy and Andy shared together. Ultimately, however, their themes are the most basic and the most universal: they are about wonder and about kindness, they are about living life with gratitude, they are about being open to the gifts of both the light and the shadow of our human experience, they are about the timeless discovery of the truth that love—despite all human fears to the contrary— really is stronger than death.

Henry A. Gustafson, B.A., B.D., S.T.M., Ph.D., is emeritus professor of New Testament at United Theological Seminary of the Twin Cities, where he taught from 1968 to 1989.

ACKNOWLEDGMENTS

I owe a debt of gratitude to many whose support made this book possible. To my law partners for graciously accepting my extended absence from the office while I wrote. To Nancy's friends, particularly Bobbi Riemenschneider, Judith Ingber, Titilayo Bediako, and Tineka Kurth, and my extended family, for including my son in their family functions and tirelessly ferrying him to piano lessons and his many other activities. To my linguist mother, Valerija Baltina-Berzina, for teaching me to love words and appreciate language. To my sister, Uve Hamilton, for offering her artistic perspective to layout and design. To Casey Feutsch, my editor, for culling the letters into a manageable number and suggesting the inclusion of "responses" to my letters from Nancy's own writings. And to my wife, Nancy, for loving me and letting me love her.

About six months before Nancy died, she gave a sermon. Not in the main sanctuary of Plymouth Congregational Church in downtown Minneapolis—Nancy wasn't an ordained minister—but in the chapel at the "early service."

Though I'm not a member of Nancy's church, I always went to hear her sermons. I'd time my arrival for after the announcements, the unison prayer, and the hymns, just before the sermon. She'd glance back to the pews near the rear door to see if I was there and wink to me as she walked to the pulpit. I'd blow her a kiss. After her talk was over, I'd motion "thumbs up" and leave.

On the occasion of this, Nancy's last sermon at Plymouth, I did not run off after she finished her talk. Not because it was her last. I had no inkling then that she would die less than six months later from the "whispering disease," ovarian cancer.

I did not rush away the moment after Nancy stepped down from the lectern because I was unable to move. I sat in the pew in the second to the last row of the chapel staring ahead. The words of the parable with which Nancy had concluded her sermon were still ringing in my ears. I saw the image of the brick wall she had painted in the parable, not the bricks of the corridor leading to the parking lot.

The parable Nancy related was set in a hospital ward. There, elderly invalids were confined to curtained beds in a sick bay. The large room on the second floor had only one window, and the woman confined to the only bed with a view out the window, Clara, became the eyes for the entire ward.

Day after day, Clara described everything she saw to the others. She painted pictures, in words, of falling leaves, sultry summer evenings, Christmas, decorations and birthday celebrations. She detailed the comings and the goings of a family across the street, giving them names and describing them so vividly that, to the others, they felt like relatives—Fran, the mother; Jimmy, the only child. Clara depicted the freckles that covered Jimmy's face in summer, guided the ward through the joys of Jimmy's first bike, evoked images of the green Teenage Mutant Ninja costume he wore at Halloween one year, the pirate outfit with scabbard he donned the next.

When Clara died, another woman was moved to Clara's bed next to the window. For the first time in the many years she had been bedridden, she would see the outside world for herself, rather than through Clara's eyes.

She turned to the window. She looked. She rubbed

her eyes. Grayish red bricks of the wall of a taller building next door filled the window from top to bottom.
Not even a glimpse of sunlight could be seen. She was
speechless.

"What's going on?" demanded the others.

She paused and took a long breath.

"Come on, tell us. Tell us what's happening out
there."

"Well," she paused. "Well, it's just like Clara said:
Jimmy's out and about on that new bike of his. He's
wearing that new birthday jacket. Clara was right:
Jimmy's hair *is* red as fire . . ."

The closing hymns were sung. The congregation
rose. I noticed people shaking hands, others hugging.
I continued to sit. For me, the walls of the chapel had
transformed into the grayish red brick of the building
adjoining the hospital. I found myself in a sick bay looking for meaning beyond what was visible. I sat questioning what was "real" and what was "imaginary."

Later that week I recounted the story to my sister
Dana. My eyes teared as I spoke of Jimmy's new red bike.
Dana, herself a psychologist, didn't lose the opportunity
to encourage self-exploration.

"What are the brick walls in *your* life?" she asked me.

Brick walls? There are no brick walls in my life, I
responded. I have a wonderful life. I married the girl
of my dreams. I love my work. I have two spectacular
children.

Dana persisted.

It was then that I, for the first time, admitted to myself that Nancy might be dying. I realized that for Nancy and me, the reality of the other side of the wall—our undying love for each other—had become our only reality. Though that part of us would live forever, there was also a hard brick wall—a physical being that could not, and would not, live forever.

This book is a compilation of letters written to Nancy after she died. The letters recount my experience of colliding with brick walls and, as well, with touching what is beyond them. Surprisingly, bumping into the "reality" beyond the brick wall opens wounds just as real as the ones from "real" walls. But, for me, the process of healing lay in being open to seeing Jimmy's red hair *and* the grayish red brick. As neither my process of experiencing the grief of Nancy's death nor writing about my presence to the two "realities" was linear, the letters, and Nancy's "responses," can be read in any order.

The letters are occasionally interspersed with writings of Nancy's that appeared in an anthology published after her death as *Gifts of Spirit: The Spiritual Legacy of Nancy Baltins*. They are reprinted with the permission of the Nancy Baltins Legacy Committee of Plymouth Congregational Church. Though "in reality" the excerpts from the anthology were written before my love letters to her, they are a response of sorts from the "reality" beyond the brick wall.

I've been asked if what is written in these letters really happened. In other words, is this book fiction or nonfiction?

Yes. And yes.

Except for Nancy's name and mine, I've changed the names of people. For simplicity, sometimes I've created "composite persons" that say or do what a number of different people actually said or did. At times, the events didn't happen in the order implied by the letters. But everything happened to me at some point.

Here are some things that are "real": Nancy Jean Solstad was born on August 9, 1945. She died on June 30, 1996. I first wrote a letter to Nancy in 1953, when we were both eight years old. I have continued writing.

AAB
Minneapolis, Minnesota

Love Letters

Dear
Nancy,

This was to be no ordinary letter. It was
to be what my group facilitator called a "grief letter."
And for such a letter, I didn't want to use just any
stationery. The legal pads, which I knew I had plenty
of in my briefcase, would clearly not do. Their yellow sheets with blue lines and a perforated edge felt
inelegant and too disposable for the letter I intended
to write to you on my flight to Boston to visit our
daughter. I'd bring the legal pads along. But they'd
be for lawyering only.

I went to your study to look through your stationery drawer. Letterhead of the *Yale Daily News*
and of the president of Smith College. How is it that
you still have that stationery thirty years after we
graduated? Did Thomas Mendenhall know, I wondered, that you somehow ended up with his official
letterhead?

Hotel stationery from Paris, Santiago de Chile,
Cairo, Salzburg. Sheets with your name imprinted
along the bottom. Notepaper with your initials

embossed on top. Eight-by-eleven-inch watermarked sheets. Four-by-six-inch note cards. Paper with scalloped edges. Different thicknesses. Varying weights. White. Cream. Beige. Peach. An unused sheaf of a gaudy pink with a red-laced border. Envelopes already stamped. Your stationery drawer overflows.

Nancy, yours was a world of communication. I yearn to enter your world. I long to communicate—to communicate with you.

This stationery, the one I finally selected, was not in your stationery drawer. It was in a thin, glossy-red box in the bottom drawer of my desk. The box still had a ribbon around it. A couple of spiral pads and a ream of copy paper lay on top of it. The box and its contents—writing paper embossed with my initials—was untouched. Too nice for business correspondence. The stationery lay unused.

I think you gave me the stationery as a gift shortly after we were married. Was it for Valentine's Day? My first birthday following our wedding? I would have been turning twenty-four. That's more than twenty-five years ago, but I can still recall lifting the lid of the box to reveal thick, cream-colored sheets of paper with my raised initials at the top. I'd never seen paper so elegant! I brushed my fingers over the embossed letters.

You told me the stationery was for thank-you notes. Thank-you notes? I'd never written one before. To whom would I write one? And for what? My friends don't know quite how to respond to even oral expressions of gratitude. "Can't you, Nancy, do them for both of us?" I asked.

For a quarter of a century you did just that—you wrote thank-you notes for both of us. And so, the box of embossed stationery went unopened. And so, too, has gone unexperienced the gift of writing a sentence or two to express gratitude.

It has taken your dying for me to run my fingers over these raised initials once again. It has taken your dying for me to acknowledge in writing the kindnesses that I'd taken for granted: the gift of a home-baked loaf of bread brought over, still warm, by your friend Denise; the gift of an offer from my friend John to take Mac bowling on a Saturday while I go for a run; the gift from my sister Dana of driving Mac to his piano lessons every Tuesday. Over the past three months, I've sent thank-you notes to friends who brought food. I've sent notes to friends of yours I have yet to meet in person. I've even sent thank-you notes to professionals who just did a job they were paid to do.

I placed two sheets of the embossed stationery in my briefcase next to the legal pads and then added half a dozen second sheets. I was ready to write my "grief letter."

"When a loved one dies, a lot is often left unsaid."

The facilitator of my grief group paused, intending that we begin considering how our own relationships were incomplete. "Dreams are left unexpressed. Hurts have gone unhealed. There's unfinished business left to complete."

Nancy, did we have unfinished "business"?

Your diagnosis was initially reported to us in positive terms. "Limited scope." "Operable." "High probability of total recovery." After returning from the doctor's office, we went for a walk around Lake Harriet. What if the news had been different? we wondered out loud as we walked the familiar path to the lake along the rose gardens. What if the news had been that you had but a week to live? Would we be doing something different than strolling arm in arm around our beloved lake?

"No," you said. "There's nothing better to do than what we've always done." We would still have stopped to admire the mallard ducks swimming in groups of six or seven, leaving V-shaped wakes. We would still have paused at the bandstand for ice cream cones and then continued walking until we could look back at the skyline of Minneapolis juxtaposed against the bucolic setting of this urban lake. You would still have ordered chocolate ice cream, I, peach frozen yogurt. We would still have held hands, you hypothesized, and we would have talked—talked, just as we did, about our children, Mac and Julia, and

about us. We would have marveled out loud about
our wonderful life together, just as we had so often
before on our walks around Lake Harriet. We had no
business to finish up in a hurry just because time was
running out, you affirmed.

I suppose "finishing business" is doing something
today that you wish you'd done differently yesterday,
before you learned how things were going to turn
out. Giving the kiss that went unkissed. Celebrating
the day that went uncelebrated. Nancy, I didn't miss
many opportunities to kiss you, did I? We did celebrate most every day, didn't we? I can see how, fifteen months ago as we walked around Lake Harriet
on the day of your diagnosis, we could have believed
we had no "unfinished business" to complete.

Now, three months after your death, I see that
what we believed on the day of your diagnosis
wasn't so. There *are* things that I would have done
differently.

Had I known you would die, I would have kissed
you even more. Had I known you would die, I would
have squeezed your hand even harder. Had I known
you would die, I would have told you even more
often how much I appreciate you, how much I love
you, how much my heart sings at the thought of you.
I would have made fewer assumptions. I would have
asked more questions. I would have cried more. I
would have made amends more often.

I would have written you thank-you notes.

Your gift to me from thirty years ago, the cream-colored, embossed stationery at the bottom of my desk drawer, has come full circle. I use it now, for the first time, to give thanks to you.

And I have so much for which to thank-you. Principal among them is this, Nancy: the wisdom that there is so much to be thankful for. You taught me that the universe is a cornucopia incessantly spilling its bounty.

At times I want to scream out against the unfairness of it all. What kind of cornucopia is this—having my soul mate die at midlife? Having our children left motherless? Then I hear your voice reminding me, "Dig deeper." There is *always* something for which to have gratitude. "Be grateful you discovered the embossed notepaper after all these years," I hear you say to me. "Brush your fingers over your raised initials again. Be grateful you've been given the opportunity to experience the wonder of writing thank-you notes. Give thanks."

I do.

Thank you for insisting that I take tap dance lessons with you. Thank you for not insisting that we go to the Symphony Ball last year. Thank you for winking to clue me in that I'd taken the bait on yet another one of your practical jokes. Thank you for having freckles that in the summer cried out for pig-

tails even when you were in your forties. Thank you
for not throwing any more surprise birthday parties
for me. Thank you for working the Sunday *Times*
crossword puzzle with me in bed until noon. Thank
you for reminding me over and over to "lighten up."

Thank you, Nancy, for being my companion.
Thank you for accompanying me on our journey together so far. And thank you for this stationery with
which I continue the journey.

with all my love,

Dear
Nancy,

"Perhaps a chair or a table."

The voice on the phone was not hostile. It was direct. Self-assured. But I sensed no judgment tied to its matter-of-fact tone.

"As a carpenter, I'd consider custom-building a chair or a table for the English," he said, using the term by which the Amish refer to non-Amish people. "But a casket. That's different. To build a casket right, a carpenter needs to have known the person well indeed."

I could tell that the voice belonged to a person who was thoughtful. A person who had contemplated life. A person who was serious about his craft. The voice belonged to a person who was decided in his views, and I knew that I would not convince the man that went with this voice to build a coffin for your body. I prodded anyway.

"I wouldn't know how to go about making a casket for a total stranger," the voice replied. "It's a job that needs to be done with reverence. How can one pay that kind of respect to someone he's never even met?"

Yet the voice seemed to identify with my search for something more fitting for you than a satin-lined brass coffin with ornate handles. Your essence was simplicity. And the voice seemed to understand that, for me, an ornamented casket was unimaginable as a resting place, even for the short period between our home and the crematorium. And so, after more prodding by me, the voice reluctantly offered an explanation to accompany the non-negotiable "No." It said, "As a child, I used to climb an oak tree near my parents' house. My sister and I would play in it for hours. We'd rubbed its bark smooth.

"When I was ten, my sister fell from that tree and suffered a concussion. She lay there, motionless, for what seemed like hours. She was pale white. I thought she was dead. I prayed there at the wide trunk of that oak, resting my forehead against its rough bark. That day, under that tree, I talked to God for the first time in my life.

"That was twenty-five years ago. I've prayed there ever since.

"Three years ago the tree died. When it died, I knew my coffin had to be made from the wood of that oak. I myself sawed off its branches. The trunk was wide and straight, and the planks came out of the mill with only a few knots. The most noticeable one was made by the branch from which perhaps my sister fell. The burled rings of that branch will pick up the stain beautifully. I'm going to use that board for the center of the lid.

"I'm only thirty-five years old," the voice continued. "I'm taking my time to build the coffin. But if needed, my partner could finish up the casket in a day or two. We keep the boards in the back of the shop. He knows just where to find them. The planks of that old oak tree are a part of me—and I'm a part of those planks. When I'm gone, the wood will speak to my partner and guide him. The casket will be finished just as if I'd done it myself."

Nancy, I still don't know the name of the person who was attached to that voice from Harmony, Minnesota. But that voice completely altered the way I would relate to your body that still lay at home in our bed.

My first reaction was disappointment and impatience. Another dead end. How can it be so difficult to find a simple wooden box? Satin-lined coffins with plush interiors. Brass fittings and ornate decorations. Coffins with stereo systems. Structures made to withstand time—not just worms and decay. Structures intended to become time capsules. These were not you! You deeply appreciated the interconnectedness of all things, the interconnectedness of the human body, the worm, the soil, the spirit.

You would not want to have your body hermetically sealed from the universe of which it was a part.

"A plain pine box," I pleaded at the mortuary service. "Just plain pine," I demanded at the crematorium with the same air of impatience I sometimes catch myself using when I'm negotiating a merger agreement with a lawyer from a large firm in New York who insists on complicating what I believe to be a simple proposal.

"No such thing," was the reply, over and over.

"No call for such things. Cremations are done in corrugated cardboard. Buryings are dignified."

Can the choices really be so limited? Does everyone accept only two options? What about the Amish? They lead a life of simplicity. Wouldn't they bury their dead in something less ornate?

I soon learned that calling the Amish is no easy task. The Amish are technology averse. Most don't have telephones. Harmony, the nearest Amish community to Minneapolis, is more than a two-hour drive. I couldn't just hop in the car and spend a day driving in hopes of finding a mortuary service or a furniture store that might have an inventory of caskets.

It was Fred's friend Brad who put me in touch with the voice from Harmony. "I've worked with a couple of master carpenters from the Amish community in Harmony," he said. "They're kind of hard to get ahold of. They don't have telephones at home. But I do know a coffee shop where some of my Amish carpenter friends have breakfast. Call there between five thirty and six o'clock in the morning. Maybe somebody can help you out."

I called with high expectations. The coffin item on the "to do" list would finally be checked off. But instead of hurrying me along the "to do" list, the conversation with the voice from Harmony permanently slowed things down, made the task even more complicated, and ultimately altered the nature of my "to do" list forever. I realized that the selection of a coffin was not a chore to be finished so that I could move on to the next one. I was meant to be present to experiencing the casket and its connection to your body. This was far too intimate a matter to leave to strangers. Just as the voice from Harmony suggested, I could no longer consider having this last resting place for your body handled just by outsiders. I had to build the casket myself.

But I had neither the tools nor the skill. I needed help. I resolved to call Fred—he was a carpenter and a master craftsman. And Fred had known both of us since childhood. He had the kind of intimacy with us about which the Amish carpenter spoke. I would enlist Fred to help me build a casket.

Fred understood the intimacy of working with wood. He didn't need me to justify my newfound

desire to be personally involved. He took on the
project eagerly. He said he'd always wanted to build
a casket. That coffin making had been considered by
medieval guildsmen to be the highest craft for the
carpenter.

Fred and I settled on the wood of a weeping willow to make your casket. I recalled how much you
admired the gracious sadness of the willow tree. Its
branches nearly touch the ground, creating an umbrella around its trunk. It reaches skyward and earth-
ward at the same time, seeming to know its maker is
found in both directions.

Though the willow was aesthetically pleasing and
though its being a *weeping* willow seemed meaningful, most important to me was that your coffin would
be made of wood, simple wood. The woods meant
so much to you. We walked the woods of our wilderness retreat often. I recall that we intuitively felt
that each of us had once existed *as* the forest. And as
we walked the forest, we felt we were reconnecting
to the fundamental elements of which we are made.
As I worked on selecting planks, measuring them to
fit, finishing them to join, I experienced this same
connection. My hands touched lumber's elements:
soil, sunshine, rain. My mind saw other elements:
the lumberjack who had felled the tree and the circular saw that had cut the plank. Does lumber have
a reality apart from its elements? I wonder. Do you,

Nancy, have a reality apart from the elements that make up who you are—your parents, your teachers, your love for the woods and my love for you?

Though I knew that you were five feet five and one half inches tall, I'd never before made something for you to fit into. Should we make the casket a foot longer? Should we leave space for the height that you *wanted* to be, not the height that you actually were?

You often told me you wanted to be taller than five foot five and a half. You loved putting on high heels. Occasionally, you'd put on shoes with spiked heels that made you five foot seven or eight. "Tall people, like you, don't understand," I recall you saying. "You take it for granted. But when you're always looking up to talk to someone, you don't take an inch or two for granted." Now I find myself assessing your body, not taking anything for granted.

Width couldn't be taken for granted either. I leaned down over your cold motionless body. Tears fell on it as I extended the tape measure to determine its exact width. Peculiar, isn't it, that in nearly fifty years I'd known you, I'd never had occasion to know the width of your body—shoulder to shoulder with arms folded across. Nancy, I came to know you in a way I had never before. It made me wonder if my appreciation of you was one-dimensional in other ways as well.

Under Fred's guiding hand, I participated in the

building project just enough. Mostly I cried. Each shaving of wood brought you to mind. Each fitting brought visions of your body lying in the casket.

At first our friends and family could not understand why I was engaged in this project. Only your godson, Chad, accepted the offer to join me. Together we measured. He helped saw. We screwed in screws. We polished. We talked about you. We listened. We listened to the saw blade. We listened to the sound of the sandpaper against the fresh wood. As we listened, we were attentive to more than pieces of wood that within a couple of days would become ashes, indistinguishable from the remains of your body.

Our friends and family couldn't help but notice the serenity with which Chad and I returned from working on the coffin. They must have seen in our faces that healing was taking place, and, eventually, your sister, your brother Jim, your nephew Billy, and your friend Therese joined us in varnishing.

Just a light coat of varnish was all that was required for the grain of the willow to show its full beauty. Just a bit of varnishing was all that was required as a healing salve for Margie, Jim, and Therese. No one could pick up the brush without acknowledging what was going on: we were building a box for your body; your body would be placed in it; it would be carried by us to the crematorium;

we would push the casket and its contents into 1,700 degree heat; then, there would be nothing left but four or five pounds of cremated remains and ashes. Nothing more.

Or is there more? Was the voice from Harmony telling us that there is more—much more?

with all my love,

Dear
Nancy,

Lipsha steals a car, follows a phantom off the road into the prairie during a blizzard, and freezes to death. Lulu is arrested by federal marshals. Fleur Pillager disappears into a snowstorm, leaving no tracks. "We should have learned not to tamper with what's beyond us," counsels the narrator. Yet, on "clear and brilliant days and nights of black stars," Fleur's tracks are "sometimes again left among us," and "it is said that she still walks."

This is what happens in the last three chapters of *The Bingo Palace*. Nancy, I read them out loud to you the night after you died. Not unlike the way we'd read the previous twenty-four chapters. Lying in bed next to you. Experiencing your presence. Glancing over at you, a bit uncertain as to whether you were truly listening. And reading on. Did you hear those chapters? Were you concerned that I was tampering with "what's beyond me"?

You died while my friend Kevin and I were up north at our wilderness retreat for the weekend. By the time I returned, the house was already filled with friends and family. A group was at your bedside, singing and praying. Another was nibbling in silence in the kitchen at a dinner laid out by my mother and Therese. Julia's friends Megan, Fran, and Katie were consoling Julia. Tom was in the backyard with Mac. I sat at your side while Jane and Therese continued to pray. I cried with Julia and Mac in my arms. I sat with my mother and the contingent in the living room. I was never alone with you.

Late that night, after Becky and Therese had tidied up the kitchen and Julia and Mac had gone to bed, I was finally alone with you. Your body was lying on our bed in the same spot where I kissed you good-bye on Friday. You were on "your" side of the bed with your head propped up the way you said eased your breathing. The comforter was pulled up to your chin. *The Bingo Palace* lay on the nightstand. Everything looked the same as I'd left it less than forty-eight hours earlier. Yet I knew that nothing, not anything, was the same. Nothing would ever be the same, ever again.

I'd last read to you the night before I left. I'm trying to remember when reading out loud became for us a daily ritual. It was just after your first bowel resection, wasn't it? My sister Dana had sent us a copy of Kaye Gibbons's *Sights Unseen*. She pleaded that we both read it right away so that the three of

us could discuss its similarities to our family dynamics before her next therapy session.

We talked about which of us would read *Sights
Unseen* first. You should, you argued, because you
read so much faster than I. I knew, though, that it
was not realistic for me to read second. If my sister's
sense of our family dynamics in *Sights Unseen* were
true, you'd never be able to contain yourself and wait
for me to finish the book before calling Dana to de-
brief. I'd be left out of the discussions, even though
they were *my* family skeletons being dismembered
and reassembled.

"No, I'll read first," I insisted.

"Why not read it out loud?" you suggested. "I
could read one chapter to you. You'd read the next
to me."

We'd been told you'd be in the hospital recovering from your surgery for at least three days. What
was the hurry? we reasoned. This was a time that we
didn't need Evelyn Wood efficiency.

The book was just as Dana had billed. We laughed,
we cried, we shared stories. We seemed to know all
the characters from personal experience. In truth,
I felt I was one of them. We stayed up well into the
night and finished the book in one sitting.

After you recovered from the surgery, I continued
to read out loud to you. In the evenings, before we
went to sleep, we'd lie down in bed, and you'd prop

up my back with a couple of pillows. At first, you'd lie on your side, looking at me while I read. After a while, you'd roll onto your back. It was then that I knew that I had to read with more emphasis, that you were ready to sleep soon, and if I were to keep your attention to the end of the chapter, I'd have to make the story compelling.

Occasionally, I'd stop reading to test if you were still awake. I'd just sit looking at you, marveling at our wonderful life together, marveling at the gift of just reading out loud to you in bed. After a moment or two of silence, you'd become alert. "I was just resting my eyes," you'd say. "Continue!" "Read!" I'd not dispute your explanation though I knew your rhythmic breathing indicated that you were not just "resting your eyes." For me it was sufficient that you were connecting to my voice and my presence. The words of the story were extra. The reading process, not the subject matter or the literary quality, made reading out loud such a rich experience.

The Bingo Palace lay on the nightstand. Unfinished. The outline of a large tent silhouetted with Christmas tree lights beckoned from the book jacket.

For a moment, I thought about taking it to the guestroom and reading there. I considered leaving it lying on the night table and finding a new book to start. Perhaps I didn't need to read at all tonight. Yet reading before going to sleep had become a ritual.

Despite all that had happened in the past twelve hours, I was sure I couldn't fall asleep without reading before I turned out the lights. And it didn't feel right to pick up a new book with just a few pages left to read of *The Bingo Palace*. *The Bingo Palace* was an unfinished chapter in my life. It was an unfinished chapter in yours. *The Bingo Palace* was *our* unfinished business.

I was drained. Too exhausted to continue an internal debate. Too exhausted to make even one more decision. I did what was most familiar. I closed the bedroom door and lay down on the bed next to you.

I tried to lie down gently on our waterbed. Yet, your body rose in a heave as I sank into the warm water-filled mattress. I looked over apprehensively from my side of the bed to yours as a wave precipitously raised your body against the edge of the bed. But there was no turning back.

I lay looking over at your body as I waited for the waves of the waterbed to subside. Your body rocked, more and more gently, until it finally came to a complete rest. My mind was flooded with thoughts of how I missed you. Knowing that you'd not tuck an extra pillow behind my back. Fear of again disturbing your body as I'd lean over to turn on the reading light. Had rigor mortis set in? I wondered. Would the heaves in the waterbed somehow damage your body?

I longed to reach over and hug you. I yearned to wrap my body around you and sleep all night nestled like spoons. I looked for any sign of movement. But you were perfectly still.

I finally picked up the book. I felt silly as I opened my mouth to start reading out loud to you. If your spirit was in the bedroom, that spirit would hear these chapters even if I read them quietly to myself, an inner voice said. "But you didn't stop reading out loud to Nancy when you knew that she'd drifted off to sleep," said another. "Don't make a fool of yourself," replied the first. "What if one of the children comes into the bedroom? How would you explain that you're reading out loud to a corpse?" Wearied by the inner dialogue, I finally began to read out loud.

I started timidly, but as I got through the first few pages, my voice gained authority. I read a chapter, stopped, and glanced over at you. You did not stir. I read louder. Tears rolled down my cheeks. I read with more emphasis. My tears baptized the pages of the book. I didn't wipe them. They marked my acceptance that you weren't just "resting your eyes" as you'd so often done before.

Tears bit into my eye sockets, their acidity burning my cheeks and blurring the ink on the page. My voice choked up as I forced myself to read through the tears. But I continued to read. My throat became sore. But I continued to read. I continued to read out loud to you until I'd finished the unfinished chapters of *The Bingo Palace*. I continued to read until I'd cried the uncried tears. I continued to read until I'd choked out the choked-up words. And then, when the last chapter was done, I was done. I fell asleep next to your body.

I was not just resting my eyes.

with all my love,

Dear
Nancy,

The light blue, late-model, full-size car
was lingering in front of our house with its lights
dimmed when Therese left at ten thirty. When your
sister Marge left at midnight, it was still there, its
engine running. Two men sat in the car, motionless,
facing forward.

"Police," I concluded. "What are *they* doing
here?" My adrenaline level, already elevated by the
news, just over twelve hours ago, of your death,
shot up higher yet. I double bolted the front door,
turned off the lights in the front rooms of the
house, and collapsed in the family room with a
glass of warm milk. It was almost one o'clock in
the morning. Tomorrow would be, as Mac likes
to say, another "big day."

As I turned off the lights in the kitchen, the
doorbell rang. The two men from the car were at our
door. In the darkness, the men appeared larger than
humans. But for the badges, which reflected the light
from the vestibule, their dark blue uniforms were

26

coextensive with the night air. I was scared. I went on the offensive.

"What do you want?" I said brusquely. "It's after midnight."

"We're . . . ah, we're from the Hennepin County Sheriff's office," one of the uniformed men responded while the two officers proffered their identification. "We're sorry to disturb you so late. But we . . . ah, we were told by the coroner's office that a death occurred here earlier today."

I was not mollified by their soft tone. "What business is it of yours?" I demanded.

"I guess the attending physician must've informed the coroner. It's routine. And usually, usually there are . . . ah, arrangements made with a mortuary. But the coroner hadn't heard yet from a mortuary. So they asked us to . . . ah, to see about the arrangements."

"Look. It's one o'clock in the morning," I stormed back. "If the coroner has any questions, have him call me in my office during normal business hours." I handed one of the deputies my business card and edged the door closed. "There anything else?" I made no effort to mask my impatience. "My wife died today. It's been a long day. I'd like to go to bed."

"I'm sorry," one of the deputies responded. "We understand, and we're very sorry about your loss. But the coroner, the coroner's got to know about the arrangements. Here's the number. Please call in the morning to let them know which mortuary service will handle the body. And it's completely your choice about, about which mortuary to use."

"If the coroner wants to talk to me, have him call my secretary and make an appointment. I'm not calling anyone. Good night."

"We apologize for . . . ah, for troubling you so late on this difficult occasion. We're sorry about your wife's death. We're just doing our job." The deputies walked down the driveway to the street.

"How can you treat someone so harshly?" I could hear your voice in my head. "You didn't have to invite them in for a cup of coffee, but you could've at least been civil. Your grief is no excuse for your behavior.

"Andy, catch them before they're gone. Apologize. Tell them you're in shock. Ask their forgiveness for treating them the way you did. Do you really want to leave this interchange with these total strangers like this? You know the law of the universe: whatever you put out, is what comes back."

Nancy, I'm sorry. I didn't heed your voice. I didn't apologize. I didn't call the coroner's office.

I was angry. I was angry you'd died. I was angry that your voice in my head was telling me to apologize and to acknowledge the karmic rules of the universe. So, rather than defuse matters with a simple call to the coroner's office, the next morning I called one of my law partners.

"Can the sheriff's office come barging into my house, demanding I hire a mortuary?" I became argumentative. "What possible compelling reason could the state of Minnesota have here? I want you to find out if there's some kickback arrangement between morticians and the coroner."

"Hold on, Andy," Eric replied. "It's me, Eric— your partner. You know I can't answer those questions. I'm sorry about Nancy's death. It is a terrible loss. Her death is an unspeakable loss for *me*. I can just imagine what it must be like for *you*. But I'm not your guy. You know we do only corporate law."

Eric tried to redirect my attention to plans for the memorial service. But I persisted. He finally promised that if I wanted, he would ask one of our law clerks to research the coroner's authority and get back to me.

Eric had not called me back by the time the deputies from the sheriff's office were at the door again that afternoon. Same car. Same uniforms. The same proffering of identification. But they were different men inside the uniforms. "We understand you've got a dead body here in the house. May we come in?"

My mind raced. Should I demand to see if they have a search warrant? Should I tell them I won't talk to them without my lawyer present?

Nancy, you'll be pleased to know that I did none of the things that raced through my mind. "Please come in," I said. "I'll take you upstairs. My wife's body is still lying in the bed where she died. It hasn't been moved."

I walked the deputies upstairs, asking the deputies not to talk business in our bedroom. "Please respect the sanctity of the space. People may be praying." I suggested that if the deputies had any further questions after they'd looked around, we could continue talking downstairs.

We entered the bedroom. Candles were lit. Debbie, Marge, and Gordon sat in chairs next to your body. Marge had a prayer book in her lap. Silence was being observed.

"So, then. What arrangements have been made to dispose of her?" asked one of the deputies, loudly breaking the silence.

"Please. If you need to talk, let's go downstairs," I whispered, ushering the deputies out. "Don't you see that these people are praying?"

Downstairs, the deputies made a half-hearted attempt to apologize for disrupting the silence. They acknowledged the grievers. They acknowledged silent prayer. But they did not acknowledge you.

You were right again, Nancy: "What comes around goes around." The deputies treated your lifeless body with the same cold dismissiveness with which I had treated their associates last night. They failed to connect to the spirit within the corpse before them, just as, yesterday, I had failed to connect to the spirit within the uniforms before me.

The deputies did not return again, leaving us, as one of them said, to "grieve in our own way." The coroner's office did not call. Eric never sent me the formal legal memorandum he'd promised, complete with references to city ordinances, state statutes, and legal precedents. But we did continue to sit with your body for another two days. We sought to provide for you a loving ambience while you were transitioning from this realm to the next. And I kept to myself that we were there to be with *you* during *your* transition, not with each other in *our* grief.

with all my love,

Dear
   Nancy,

From the moment Betsy noticed that you'd stopped breathing Sunday morning, your body had not been left alone. Betsy sat with you, singing lullabies. Julia, Mac, and Marge knelt at the foot of the bed and wept. Friends arrived. They, too, ended up drawn to our bedroom. By the time I returned from our wilderness retreat late Sunday afternoon, candles had been lit and surrounded the bed. Occasionally, hymns or spirituals were being softly chanted.

At dinnertime, Marge and Therese whispered that they'd prefer to eat after the others had finished. They continued to sit at your side in silence with candles lit and tiptoed out of the room only after Chad returned from dinner. Chad left the room only after I was at your side. A sort of vigil had been informally established. There was an unspoken sense that leaving the bedroom unattended would amount to abandoning *you*, not just your body. Like novitiates in an esoteric religious order, we were supporting you in whatever mysterious transition you were making, without understanding what we were doing or why.

Last night, I had fallen asleep at your side. Sleep was an inevitable endpoint to finishing the unfinished chapters of *The Bingo Palace,* of crying the uncried tears. Sleep had not been a mindful choice.

When I woke, candles were no longer burning. Spirituals were no longer being chanted. But the aura in our bedroom was unchanged. I knew then that the presence of your spirit was not an illusion intensified by the churchlike atmosphere. I looked over at your body. Though it was gray and immobile, an aliveness permeated its skin. During the night, it appeared to have become diaphanous. Inexplicably, while your body became more rigid, its boundaries appeared less defined. A sort of luminous radiance emanated from it.

I hadn't eaten since lunch on Sunday. Though it was before five o'clock in the morning and still dark outside, I was hungry. I heard Marge moving around in the guestroom and asked her to come sit with you while I went downstairs to eat.

Lapsam was already making breakfast. He cupped his hands together at his chest, his fingertips perfectly aligned, and bowed, one vertebra at a time, his eyes fixed on me. As was his custom, Lapsam acknowledged my presence without saying a word.

I hunched my shoulders. Briefly lowered my head. I made no attempt to replicate Lapsam's deliberateness.

I'd mechanically bowed my head to Lapsam ever since he came to live with us as an informal day nurse a couple of months before you died. At first, I think I viewed the bow as a Tibetan handshake. It took me a couple of weeks to realize that there was more. When he bowed, Lapsam looked at me as if he were discovering something within me. His quality of undivided attention seemed to suspend time. I felt at once investigated and adored. He'd not just greeted me or acknowledged my presence. He'd somehow sanctified the space.

Lapsam had just recently arrived from Dharamsala. He said he was eager to learn English and "Western ways." But I sensed that Lapsam would perceive my shaking his hand as a sign of aggressiveness, not graciousness. I kept returning his bow.

Lapsam spoke little. He moved quietly. He removed his shoes at the door, replacing them with delicate slippers made of reed and silk, and walked as if each step was a conscious decision. His loose-fitting kimono barely moved as he glided across the floor.

Lapsam ate in silence. He drank tea in silence. He'd pause to observe the appearance of the boiling water before methodically removing the pot from the range. I'd see him look at the change in the color of the water as the tea steeped. He'd observe the heat rise from the pot. He'd slowly pour the tea from the pot into the cup, watching the liquid momentarily suspended in midair. He would wait for the tea to settle in the cup. Then, he would lift the cup to his lips, cradling it gently in both hands. The tea would rest in his mouth before he swallowed it. For Lapsam, drinking tea was a ceremony.

Lapsam talked like he made tea—deliberately, responding to my questions about Tibetan ways with enigmatic epithets that were often more in the nature of questions, not answers. I was struck by how many times the questions he posed had no evident answers. I reasoned that, in part, his English was too broken. In part, my understanding of Eastern culture too primitive. But, though I'd often not understood his point intellectually, I usually felt closure. With him, things made sense without my understanding why.

After finishing breakfast in silence, I approached Lapsam. "I've experienced a numinous presence emanating from Nancy's body since her death," I told him. "Isn't what I'm experiencing something like what Tibetans understand to happen after death?"

"Whatever experience you have, that *is* your experience." Lapsam bowed. "These things, they do not depend on mind—what mind understand. Your own experience—that is guide."

Lapsam paused. He sat motionless, looking into

my eyes. He must have seen the pain behind them.
He continued without my having to ask that he explain further. "Guidance we have from teachers—our
Tibetan teachers—is just one path. Tibetan path is
not Truth."

"But your tradition *does* teach that there is a life
after death," I pushed. "Do you believe that the next
life happens right away? I noticed yesterday that you
bowed and recited chants whenever you were in the
presence of Nancy's body. It seemed like you were
communicating *with* Nancy. Do you think she's already reincarnated?"

"We offer blessing to *all* sentient beings," he responded. "And we pray negative influences in *all* sentient beings be purified and transformed."

"Does the chant you were reciting have a meaning?"

"*Om Mani Padme Hum?* Just syllables. In Pali. No
specific meaning. But I am not master. I not understand what I not know from my own experience. I
just practice."

Despite his protestations, after more prodding
from me, Lapsam did clarify that the mantra *Om
Mani Padme Hum* is the mantra of compassion.
Though, technically, its six syllables have no meaning, they embody the entire Tibetan teaching on
compassion and are intended to dispel suffering in
the six realms of samsara—the cycle of birth and rebirth. Rebirth in samsara is averted by reciting the

mantra. The *bardo* of "dying" is the last opportunity
for such purification.

"What *is* a *bardo*?" I asked.

Lapsam cautioned again that he was not a master
and that he felt inadequate to explain. I begged. He
relented. What I remember from our conversation
is that there are four *bardos:* "birth/rebirth," "this
life," "death/dying," and "after death." He said that
bardos are not discrete events and describe a process
that is permeable at the edges. A *bardo* is without
substance, he said, the word *bardo* literally meaning
"gap" or "in between."

"So you mean that life and death are not distinct
events?" I asked.

"*Bardo* is like night turn into day," replied
Lapsam. "Day unfold gradually, become more and
more manifest, until eventually sun is blazing in the
sky. 'Death/dying' and 'after death' are similar."

I glanced at the cover page of the *Star Tribune*.
"Sunrise - 5:31 a.m.," I read in the upper right-hand
corner. I looked at my watch. It was 5:15. But outdoors, night had already completely yielded. Lapsam
had turned off the fluorescent lamp over the sink
and was washing dishes in natural light. I bowed
to Lapsam, my hands cupped at my chest, and went
back upstairs to our bedroom. Marge was at your
side, her hand resting on your rigid knee.

I sat down next to Marge and continued to reflect

on the possibility of a soft boundary between "this life" and "after death." I could see that your physical body was transforming into something harder and more colorless. But something else in the room was becoming softer and brighter. The light body that was present in our bedroom felt fragile. A mysterious process seemed to be occurring to your body. I knew I had to be present while the inexplicable unfolded.

What Lapsam and I did not talk about is taboos. But I think he would have acknowledged that different cultures deal with the dying in different ways. Here the cultural norm is distance from dead bodies. I suspect Lapsam would have affirmed that there is no right or wrong way. But my conversation with Lapsam helped me understand that tradition is less important than presence of mind.

That evening, I lay down in our bed deliberately. One vertebra at a time. I looked over at your body the way Lapsam looks at me when he is bowing. Your presence filled the room. I let its numinous energy wash over me. It felt like entering a waterfall. Misty at first. Then droplets of water. Finally a downpour that drenched every part of my being. I was immersed. I fell asleep. That night, sleep was not the inevitable endpoint of a thoughtless sequence that started with something else.

with all my love,

Dear
Nancy,

Last Sunday night I was making a list of
the chores I still had to finish that week, when your
friend Giselle stopped by. I made polite conversation
with her for as long as I could. But as you know, for
me that's not long with Giselle, and after a couple of
minutes, I tried to escape by telling her I had to do
the wash.

Giselle wasn't put off. She said she'd help me with
the laundry. I was cornered. I was stuck with her
once again, dreading yet another conversation about
some New Age guru she was sure had the key to the
world's problems (and also aware of your voice in
my head, reminding me that my visceral reaction to
Giselle was evidence that Giselle was mirroring issues
of my own).

Though I knew you would have encouraged me
to explore my "energy" around Giselle, I was in no
mood for self-exploration. I proceeded with Giselle
to the laundry room without my having even considered using the occasion as an opportunity to form

sympathetic feelings for those who may be impatient with *my* worldviews. (I think I justify that my being a successful corporate lawyer assures that others must view me as well grounded, notwithstanding such things as my keeping your body present after your death.)

We were folding laundry when Giselle launched into a monologue about astral planes. She pontificated about how the spirit passes through certain "planes" after the death of the body and, with an authoritative voice, declared that you were now in the sixth astral plane.

"How do you know?" I asked to humor Giselle. "Seems to me like those are some pretty uncharted waters to make such a categorical pronouncement."

"I talk to her," replied Giselle.

"You do what!" I let one of Mac's shirts drop.

"I've been guiding her," Giselle continued. "Nancy was passing though the fourth plane last night—it's the plane of disembodied spirits. And before a spirit can move on to the higher planes, it must pass through this plane of disembodied spirits. If a person's spirit gets caught there, it's trapped among the disembodied spirits forever, unable to go back into the body she left or forward into a new body. That's why it's important to have a guide."

"And you're a licensed guide?" I made no attempt to hide my cynicism.

Giselle apparently decided not to interpret my question as an insult and responded by describing her own travels through astral planes. She'd traveled "out of body" five separate times, she said. I listened somewhat attentively to the first few, but after the fourth recounting of a luminous sphere and pulsating golden white light, I returned to worrying about the chores that had to be done: I had to remind Roberta to pick up the dry cleaning. What about a birthday present for my mother? Would your sister Jane expect that I buy birthday presents for her twins? I was already a day late in watering the plants. I could squeeze in watering them tomorrow, after driving Mac home from his karate lesson, I reasoned. But that was the time I'd set aside to organize your spiritual papers for Howard, who was to come by for them in a week. What am I doing listening to Giselle carry on about astronaut planes, or whatever they're called?

I was wondering if it would insult Giselle for me to go to my study for a pencil and a pad to jot down my list, when Giselle's voice reentered my consciousness. "Nancy wants you to know that your feeling overwhelmed has to do with you, not the chores," I heard Giselle saying.

"Excuse me," I stopped folding the laundry. "Did you say you think my chores are overwhelming me?"

"I've got no idea," she replied. "You certainly give

the outward appearance of having it all together. But I wouldn't be surprised if you were overwhelmed. I imagine that's a pretty customary reaction for someone whose wife died just two months ago. Frankly, I don't know how you manage to stay on top of everything with Julia, Mac, the house, and your job.

"But I'm just repeating to you what Nancy told me when I talked to her yesterday."

"What?" Giselle now had my full attention.

"I didn't get the sense that Nancy was worried." Giselle didn't acknowledge my surprise. "She was just making a statement of fact. She said being overwhelmed comes from within you, not from what's going on outside."

"You talk to Nancy? How do you do that?"

"Talking is straightforward," Giselle replied. "It's identifying the obstacles in the astral planes from here, and holding her lovingly through them, that requires care. If you want to talk to Nancy, all you have to do is listen. The universe will speak to you with her voice."

"Just listen?" I did not hide my disbelief. "I'm listening. I don't hear Nancy."

"I don't want this to sound rude. But you weren't listening to *me* just now. Your body was here but your mind was racing off somewhere else. Your soul was not connected to your mind *or* to your body. Though your body and brain may have acted awake, your *being* was totally asleep. To hear, *you* must be awake."

Suddenly I was interested in what Giselle had to say. I wanted to learn about the possibility of communicating directly with you. I felt embarrassed that I'd been impertinent with Giselle and tried to defend my behavior.

"It may have looked like I drifted off a bit," I said. "But in my line of work you learn to listen and think at the same time." As I was uttering the words, I could tell that Giselle knew, as did I, that they were contrived. I tried again. "Tell me about being awake."

Giselle put a pile of folded clothes on the counter and sat down. "I suppose you've heard the Sufi story of Nasrudin and the lost key," Giselle asked rhetorically. I nodded affirmatively. But Giselle proceeded to recount the story anyway.

In the story, Nasrudin is on his hands and knees searching for a lost key. A friend of his walks by.

"Nasrudin," says the friend. "I see you're looking for something. Can I help?"

"I've lost my key," replies Nasrudin.

"Where exactly did you lose it?" asks the friend.

"Over there by the tree."

"But then why are you searching for it here by the streetlight?"

"Because there's more light over here," replies Nasrudin.

Giselle is right: the story of Nasrudin and the lost key is my story. I search for answers where there is light—even when I intuitively know the answers aren't there. I bemoan my never-ending chores. But I'm afraid to look for relief from my chores, or from my reactions to them, in places where, for me, it's dark. Giselle accused me of liking to stay in my comfort zone—managing things by myself, acting as if I'm on top of everything, never revealing my vulnerability. Not being open to messages from you. Not talking to you.

"Paradoxical as it sounds," Giselle continued, "waking up is moving from the light into the dark. Waking up is being willing to leave the comfortable areas of our lives and beginning to explore the dark places. Does that make sense to you?" Giselle asked.

I reminded Giselle that you and I had been to a Jungian therapist. We'd worked on getting in touch with our "shadows." But, I confessed, I'm confused about how all that applies to my communicating with you, Nancy.

Giselle didn't explain. She did keep talking. Could it really have been for an hour? In any event, what I concluded from her monologue is that it's an attitude—a way of seeing reality by being open to things that aren't completely illuminated. Listening, she said, including listening to you, Nancy, requires being willing to be receptive—receptive to not just the spoken word, or even to "body language," but to communications whose origins are completely unclear.

I was not satisfied. But it was late—and I know Giselle is capable of talking all night. So I feigned understanding by nodding my head more frequently while she talked, and, eventually, she seemed satisfied that I had heard her and bid me good night.

Before going to bed, I checked the computer for e-mail messages. Though Julia rarely communicates from college by e-mail and I had not said anything to her about being overwhelmed, that evening a message from Julia awaited me:

"It's OK, Dad, to feel overwhelmed. This whole process of grieving is overwhelming. Trying to take care of everything is exhausting. Everything will work out just fine.

"Dad, don't hesitate to ask people to help you to do small tasks. Everyone is eager to help you in any way they can."

I was incredulous that Julia would "happen" to write me at this particular moment. I wondered what inspired her. But I took her unsolicited advice. Believe it or not, I actually called Giselle. Now *there's* looking for solutions in my areas of darkness! Right, Nancy?

"I was kind of disappointed you denied feeling overwhelmed when I stopped by." Giselle gave no indication of surprise that I'd called her. "I kept hoping that you might ask for help.

"In fact, I was kind of hoping that you'd ask me to go through Nancy's spiritual papers and put them in order. I know she has a ton of them. Is organizing them something you've ever thought about having someone do? I'd love to take on that project."

I accepted her offer, thanked Giselle, and mentally checked off one of the items on my list of things to do. It didn't occur to me at the time to also thank you.

I do that now, Nancy. Thank you.

with all my love,

from *Gifts of Spirit;* chapel meditation,
October 14, 1990

. . . Paul says:

> *The Lord is at hand. Have no anxiety about*
> *anything but (be) in prayer and supplication.*
> *With Thanksgiving, let your requests be made*
> *known to God, and the peace of God which*
> *passes all understanding will keep your heart*
> *and mine in Christ Jesus.*

In reading those words, I was reminded of a particular situation when I followed this counsel. My husband and I have a son, Mac, who has Down syndrome.
When he was tested for first grade, the results were
such that he was invited into a mainstream school
situation. The first year was rocky and stressful, but
he managed to pass to second grade. There we met a
teacher who had great expectations, which Mac took
great pleasure in flouting. He is prone to do this with
anyone he feels does not really like him. On the teacher's notes home to us, Mac would sit on the sidewalk
in front of the house and erase the sad faces made by
the teacher to communicate misbehavior and change

them to happy faces. I thought this pretty clever. The teacher was not amused.

And the hearing aides for his minimal hearing loss had not helped him enough so that he was invested in wearing them. Instead he would leave them at school, hide them, even try to throw them away. I finally gave up trying to make him wear them.

When my husband and I went into our fall conference, I was stunned. Instead of the usual four people, there were thirteen professionals waiting for us—to lower the boom, I thought. It was time for Mac to go join his own kind in the self-contained classroom. I felt extremely anxious to get this conference over and stop fighting battles with and for Mac.

The social worker turned to the woman on his left, introducing her as the hearing specialist for the entire district and asked her to begin. I realized I had been praying ever since I entered the room. "Dear God, please help me get through this without breaking down. Dear God, please help me to stay cool." I even got down to details. . . .

The hearing specialist turned away from me and addressed the rest of the team. "I agree with Mrs. Baltins" were the words out of her mouth. "I don't believe that Mac's hearing aids are necessary for him to wear." The universe stood still and then tilted on its axis. As she went on and the rest went on—I realized they were not there to accuse or confront me or my husband. They were all there to confront and support the classroom teacher to let her know that Mac was there to stay, and she better figure out how to get along with him.

The peace of God flooded my being. It was the first time I really believed that the real world did want to count Mac in. I didn't have to personally be there to make it happen. I didn't have to try to live forever.

Dear
Nancy,

First my cousins, Evan and Linda. Next
your brother's family from Kentucky. Then my
mother, my sister Dana, Chad, and your friend
Becky. Lastly your sisters, Marge and Jane. They
have now all departed from our wilderness retreat
to return to town, leaving Julia, Mac, and me alone
with your friend Therese and her husband, Gary,
to integrate the rituals that unfolded here earlier
today—experiencing the sanctuary of these woods
as we walked the two miles to Spring Lake Creek in
silence, carrying your cremated remains, watching
your scattered ashes disappear in our tiny creek on
their journey to the Mississippi, reciting prayers and
singing spirituals at the foot of the Yazzie sculpture,
having me wash, one by one, the hands of the friends
and family that joined us here to bid your tangible
presence good-bye. It is now night. Mac, Julia, and
I collapse in the red Adirondack chairs on the deck.
"What a day," Mac exclaims. No one responds. We
gaze at the star-studded sky.

In these northern woods of Wisconsin, the
stars appear brighter and more numerous than in
Minneapolis. The sky seems blanketed by them as
if they were bright grains of sand in an immense in-
verted beach. No, not even grains of sand, I think
to myself. Grains of sand are still separate particles.
What I see is completely undifferentiated. It is not so
much the individual stars that sparkle. The sky as an
entirety seems to shimmer and pulsate.

As my body begins to mold to the shape of this
Adirondack chair that held you so often, I find myself marveling at the capacity of my cerebral cortex
to reinterpret data to fit my learned views of reality.
I've been taught that the stars are massive discrete
spheres of distant burning gas. They appear tiny
only because they are far away. I know they're not
close together but separated by immense expanses
of empty space.

But this is not what my eyes apprehend. My eyes
experience a homogeneous milky ceiling that is just
beyond the reach of my outstretched hand. As I sit
on our deck in silence, gazing skywards at my learned
vision of the Milky Way, I wonder if my experience
of the loss of you, Nancy, is also being reinterpreted
by my brain to fit a learned worldview.

"Remarkable sky, isn't it," I say to Mac, who is
seated on the chair next to me. "The stars seem to

sparkle differently than I've ever noticed before.
I wonder if it has something to do with Mom."

"The sky doesn't have s-something *to do* with
Mom," replies Mac. "The sky *is* Mom."

"Is that what you experience?" I ask. "Or is it
what you see?"

"I don't understand," he replies. "W-what's the
difference?"

Nancy, I've got so much to learn from Mac.
Over and over he reminds me that analyzing and
reasoning interfere with my ability to see the unfolding of miracles. He has prodded me to discard
my sophistication in favor of a childlike acceptance.
And, on occasion, when I have followed his lead, I,
too, have been able to experience the magical world
in which he lives—a world in which a simple toy
provides hours of entertainment; a world in which
everyone, not just persons who fit within the concept
of friends and family, is embraced with a full hug; a
world in which each caterpillar is seen anew, a fresh
experience of furry movement untainted by prior
observations.

Despite all the modeling we've had from Mac
on not clinging to expected outcomes, I must admit,
Nancy, that, all too often, I still find myself overcome
by my attachment to desired results. How desperately
I wish you were here on the Adirondack chair beside
me. How profoundly I desire that a year ago were

frozen in time. Intellectually, I know that everything is impermanent. Experientially, I know that the tighter I squeeze, the more evanescent the object of my squeezing becomes, and the more I ease my grasp, the more my experience becomes alive. Yet, some part of me continues to want to hold on.

I'm not sure that as you breathed your last breath, I would have been able to ease my grip on the outcome to which I was attached—your living—and stay present to your dying. Nancy, I'm afraid that my yearning to have you alive at my side forevermore might have overpowered me, and I would have been unable to let go completely. I realize that I might not have been able to softly sing lullabies to you as you died, as Betsy did. Would even a subtle clinging by me have paralyzed the space in which you were about to undergo a life transition—a transition, like any, that needs openness and freedom?

Did some deep inner part of you suspect that I would not have been able to be free of grasping as you died? Did some inner guide know that I would succumb to attachment to outcomes at this crucial moment when you were about to make a metamorphosis that needed complete freedom? Is that why you encouraged me to come up here to our wilderness retreat last weekend with my friend Kevin—so that you could die without any clinging energy from me impeding your path?

The news of your peaceful death in Betsy's soft presence reached me here while Kevin and I were preparing to depart on Sunday morning to return to Minneapolis. "We got the call," said Kevin. He didn't have to add a substantive explanation. The news was in his eyes.

Nancy, you will be gratified to learn that I did not grasp at rushing back to Minneapolis upon hearing the news of your death. After collapsing into Kevin's arms, I sank down onto the bench by the lake and stared at the Yazzie sculpture. From that angle, looking across the bay, its massiveness is dwarfed by the grove of red pine at the shoreline. The sculpture's two ten-foot figures, united in a gentle caress, appear almost whimsical against the backdrop of pines reaching skyward for over a hundred feet.

I am reminded of how you delighted in the juxtaposition created by the sculpture's softness emanating from hard stone. The expressions on the faces of the gunmetal gray torsos are somber, yet gentle. They gaze across the lake with a tender resignation. The intertwined figures appear to have both a hard and a soft body. As I sat looking at the two linked figures, I was reminded that at the installation of the sculpture you reflected aloud that the figures seemed to represent us. We, too, were intertwined, you said— appearing separate but made of just one slab of the same solid substance.

Just five days ago, I experienced your body, like the Yazzie sculpture, as having both hard and soft components. I thought I knew your hard body so totally. I considered it impossible for me to ever forget its physical sensation. From time to time, I remember closing my eyes and slowly moving my fingers over your cheeks, nose, eyes, and forehead, over and over. I was memorizing your face with my fingertips, just in case I were ever to be blinded. I held your scalp in my cupped hands. I locked my legs with yours.

But there was more. There was a presence that did not depend upon my seeing or touching you. There was a presence that emanated when you entered the room and I was dead asleep. There was a presence that I felt in my fingertips before they touched your skin. There was a soft body that was just as palpable as the hard one. Did the soft body depend upon the hard body? I wondered as I sat looking at the Yazzie sculpture. Was I capable of deepening into my experience of your soft body without the hard body to give it substance? Would my experience of you after your death be like the Yazzie sculpture in reverse—an inexplicable hardness emanating from your softness? But I sensed that clinging even to a metaphor would promote suffering. I rose to leave.

I did not rise to leave for Minneapolis, however. I rose to walk to Spring Lake Creek. Kevin walked with me through these woods that you had walked

without exception every time we came here. You
often recounted to me how you marveled at the
sound of the wind in the trees. You noticed the iridescent colors of the dragonflies that hover above the
marshy pond in the heat of the summer. You regaled
us with news of the tracks of the muskrat, beaver,
and titmouse in the fall. You delighted in the yellow
flag iris, juneberry, Canada mayflower, and wild sar-
saparilla along the trail interspersed between the five
varieties of wild fern you had identified. You admired
the bubbling water of the creek during even the cold-
est winter months, when the trail was passable only
on cross-country skis. You appreciated its blue black
heaviness against the white snow in the winter and
its exuberant azure blue in the summer. You commented on its consistently energetic force.

Though Spring Lake Creek was your destination,
it was not your objective. Your objective was being
in the sanctuary of the woods, listening to its choral
music—the wind. The wind could be heard before it
could be seen, I recall your saying. It could be seen
before it could be felt. Only after hearing and seeing
did the wind manifest itself to the touch.

As I walked with Kevin to the creek last Sunday
after we learned that you had died, I began to realize
that we were meant to return here this weekend. The
Yazzie sculpture and the trail to Spring Lake Creek
are sacred places. Sacred to you, sacred to your spirit,

sacred to our ongoing experience of your presence in
our lives. And so, Nancy, I am back here, only five
days later, with the cremated remains of your body
in a Grecian urn—an urn you and I purchased in
Corinth more than a dozen years ago. It feels like
a lifetime ago. Nancy, it was a lifetime ago.

Julia, Mac, and I will depart early tomorrow
morning, leaving Therese and Gary here to be further healed by the serenity of these woods. Since
they will remain here alone for the next three days,
I will not be the one to check and recheck the lights
and windows before departing. I will not meticu-
lously put this place, which you and I adore so much,
in my customary protective bubble. Nancy, I am practicing not clinging. Perhaps in the last moments of
our next lifetime together, you will not again have
to send me away.

with all my love,

*Dear
Nancy,*

This year, Mac's fall piano recital was not
held in the practice studio. Mrs. Reed had somehow
arranged with Hamline University to make available
a small auditorium in Sundin Hall for her Suzuki
method students. The small balcony in the rear, the
ornate chandelier, and the painted reliefs on the ceiling raised my expectations—I felt we were in a concert
hall for performances by accomplished pianists. I was
anxious for Mac. Was this above his level?

After being introduced by Mrs. Reed, and bowing
to the audience, but before sitting down to play, Mac
paused. Not just for a moment or two. He appeared
to be frozen on the stage at the side of the piano.
I sensed the audience begin to fidget. Mrs. Reed
glanced over at me. I raised my eyebrows question-
ingly. She gently cleared her throat and looked quizzically at Mac.

Mac was unfazed. He was looking at the area
where I was sitting. But he didn't appear to be
looking at me. His eyes were riveted at the empty

seat next to me. Finally, he bowed his head and approached the piano. Seated at the piano, with his hands poised over the keyboard, he paused again. This time, with his back facing me, I couldn't tell if he still appeared to be in a trance. I heard him take a deep breath. He began to play Arietta by Mozart.

His short fingers danced over the keys melodically during the leggiero. He lifted himself from the seat during the forte. His body's mass appeared to flow from his chest through his hands and on to the keyboard. His head was bowed during the pianissimo. Thrown back in playful abandon in the allegro. Mac had become a physical extension of the changing rhythms of this whimsical piece by Mozart.

After the recital, I pushed through the crowd of parents and students to get to Mac, who was already at the punch bowl. "Mac, you were terrific," I gushed. "You played like I've never heard before. You *became* the music." I told him that the audience was so completely captivated, that he got everyone's attention at the beginning, even before he played a single note, by standing on the stage in what looked like a trance.

"What was going on?" I asked.

"M-M-Mom," he replied. "She was in the seat next to you. I c-c-couldn't stop looking at her."

While others left for the reception hall to eat chocolate chip cookies and lemon bars, Mac sat down next to me and patiently explained that you, Nancy, *always* come to his recitals. Mac says you smile to let him know not to worry. He waits for you to nod and wink at him before he sits down to play. He knows that even if he makes a mistake, you'll love him. "I waited and waited for Mom to nod today," he said. "I couldn't make her out." And when he finally could, Mac explained, you also blew him a kiss.

Nancy, you must have sat with Mac every day, sometimes twice a day, playing "Lightly Row," "Twinkle, Twinkle Little Star," "Mary Had a Little Lamb," and Schumann's "The Happy Farmer." Cheering him on, you fingered the simple Suzuki melodies on the piano, you hummed them for him when you walked with him. You played them on the tape deck in the car. At times I couldn't get the singsong tunes out of my head. I thought that our entire lives were being suffocated by Suzuki. But you, you never tired. Your patience never seemed to be exhausted as you pulled Mac along at his own methodical pace.

A couple of weeks ago, during a lesson, Mrs. Reed commented that sometimes she didn't know how much of Mac's piano playing is Mac and how much of it is you. "I have a hard time telling where Nancy leaves off and where Mac starts," she said. "Nancy was so much a part of Mac's musical development. I'm wondering if we shouldn't think about trying something a little different—more emphasis on reading music, not just listening and repetition in the traditional Suzuki method."

I talked to Mac about learning to read music. "With Mom gone, there's just not as much music in the house to be heard," I said. "You'll have to develop your eye as well as your ear."

"That's cool," responded Mac. "But I'll still listen to Mom, too. We'll d-d-do both."

Now it is time for me to bow to you, Nancy. Not just at piano recitals but also when I sit down to practice with Mac. When I take Mac to his karate classes. When I attend parent-teacher conferences. When I plan Mac's schedule, which without you often seems to require not just one but three or four adults in addition to me. When I marvel at the remarkable accomplishments of this boy with Down syndrome and ask where you leave off and Mac begins.

with all my love,

Dear
Nancy,

I finally got around to stopping by the church to pick up the photographs that were displayed at the reception in Jackman Hall after your memorial service. The picture display was your sister Jane's idea. The photographs of you were selected by Margie, Julia, and Jane with little involvement from me.

I arrived at the church to discover two large boxes filled with photographs. Had they all really been displayed at the reception after the memorial service? I wondered. I only remembered the large oil portrait of you painted by your brother Jim when you were nineteen years old.

The portrait was back in my office when I returned to work the following week. Jane or Margie must have picked it up after the service and rehung it. I never noticed it had been removed. Nor had I noticed any of the other pictures displayed in Jane's collage.

The boxes were not wrapped with holiday paper.

They weren't tied with ribbons interlaced with holly.
Yet opening them was Christmas. Photographs of
you when you were a toddler. A picture of you as
the Snow Queen in sixth grade at Kenwood School.
Pictures of you graduating at Northrop School.
There was a picture of the two of us in costume for
Charley's Aunt, in which we played the romantic
leads as Jack Chesney and Kitty Verdun when we
were fifteen. Wedding pictures—including the picture of you with your hair teased and ringlets along
the sides of your face. I remember that you so dis-
liked that picture, even though it made you look like
a movie star. It was "fake looking," you said. I recall
your threatening to destroy the negative. Yet, to your
dismay, your mother sent it to the *New York Times*
for the wedding announcement. Now, here it was
again at your memorial service.

I sifted through a couple of black-and-white
"artsy" photographs of you that I'd taken when I
attended a photography course at the Minneapolis
College of Art and Design. How did Margie and
Jane find those pictures? I wondered. It's been more
than twenty-five years since I've seen them.

I must admit, Nancy, that I couldn't help thinking
that my "fine art" portraits of you weren't half-bad—
for a lawyer dabbling in art photography. I remember
developing them in the darkroom at MCAD and
seeing your face slowly appear through the chemical

bath. I remember noticing your high cheekbones and winsome smile—playing with the contrasts to bring out more of the drama in your eyes. I was struck by your beauty then. I was struck by your beauty again as I sat with the boxes of photographs.

Did I tell you, while you were alive, often enough how beautiful I found you, Nancy? I'm afraid I may have fallen short. Forgive me. I may have taken for granted that you knew how much I appreciated your physical beauty as well as the beauty of your soul and heart. Let me say it again now, Nancy: you are beautiful; Nancy, I love you.

As I went through nearly fifty years of photographs, I kept marveling at how unchanged you were. At five and at fifty, there was something unmistakably *you* in those pictures. You never lost your impish look even in the most formal of the pictures. In some portraits, I could see you had tried hard, to no avail, to mask your whimsical streak of naughtiness. Paradoxically, your deliberate attempt to hide that streak seemed to me to make it all the more pronounced.

You loved having photographs displayed around our house. Every desk, every table, every radiator cover, every credenza, every nightstand, every commode had photographs of family—your parents and mine, your siblings and mine, Julia, Mac, you, me. There were too many, I remember thinking.

Occasional pictures of our parents and siblings, I could understand these. Pictures of relatives that had died or didn't live with us, they served as a reminder.

But Julia, Mac, you, and me? We saw them and each other every day. We didn't need reminders of ourselves, I recall reasoning with you. "How about keeping more of the family photographs in picture albums and putting out some of the art stored in the attic? Many of the pictures don't even qualify as photographs. They're just snapshots," I argued.

"Do you see how different Julia looks in that prom picture?" you'd respond. "It was taken just a year ago, and she's already completely changed. We're all in constant metamorphosis. I need the pictures for some sense of continuity."

You'd continue. "The Julia that's in that picture from a year ago isn't alive anymore. That Julia died when she was sixteen, the same year the picture was taken. Look at her then: she was so eager, so unworldly. The Julia that lives with us today is a completely different Julia. I don't love her any more or any less. But now she's sophisticated. She's poised. I love seeing both the Julia that has died and the Julia that is alive upstairs in her bedroom."

Of course your reasoning prevailed. The photographs remained in the rooms, blanketing every open space. The artwork remained in the attic. And our gallery of photographs has remained frozen in the

state it was when you died. No new pictures have
been added. The Julia and Mac you knew have died.
I need to put up some recent pictures of them to remind myself of who they were and where they came
from four months ago when they, like I, were in
shock.

The toddler Nancy, the graduate student Nancy,
the therapist Nancy. They died years ago. The Nancy
that died of ovarian cancer, she died just months
ago. The box of photographs reminds me that your
deaths have been going on for a lifetime. Though
now unphotographable, the essence of you that is so
pronounced in pictures from the age of five to fifty,
that essence still continues, doesn't it?

with all my love,

Dear
Nancy,

Yesterday, as I was walking back to my office, I became hypnotized by a window display that was being changed at the Dayton's store downtown. An overstuffed leather couch, with scrolled legs that matched an elaborately carved Victorian table, was being removed. Blue and yellow striped vinyl beach chairs and a bleached canvas umbrella were being rearranged in their place. A man in bib work overalls was casually holding a mannequin under his arm as if it were weightless.

I noticed a tall, somber image in a navy-blue overcoat and plaid Black Watch scarf reflected in the window. Like me, the image was carrying a briefcase. But the briefcase appeared to contain a yellow pail with a red plastic shovel and rake set. Confused, I momentarily glanced down at the briefcase in my hand to confirm who I was. When I looked back at the images in the pane of glass, the illusion of the window display had been broken. It had become a staging area where two separate worlds overlapped, with stiff mannequins vying for the same space as "real" workmen and my "unreal" reflection.

I wasn't paying attention to where I was walking, and I collided with a lady wearing an immense hat. Its brim struck my cheek, and I was momentarily concerned that I had knocked the hat off the lady's head. I instinctively reached up with my arm to catch the hat's anticipated fall and nearly hit the woman again with my briefcase.

"I'm sorry. You OK?"

The woman responded with a warm smile, the softness of her light brown eyes melting the iciness of the winter air. This would not be a "hit and run" encounter.

"I guess I found myself a bit disoriented," I said. "Beach chairs? Mannequins in Speedo bathing suits? They seem so out of place here in this subzero weather."

The woman nodded meaningfully as if I'd said something profound. "No damage done." And as she turned her attention back to the window, she added, "It's never easy to know who we are or where we're going."

It was only then that I observed the hat that I'd grazed with my cheek. It was an elaborate Carmen Miranda "Chiquita Banana" affair. The stiff brim supported little figurines in the shape of palm trees and fruits. A colorful drawing of a beach against a

light blue ocean was enhanced by real sand in the
shape of miniature castles outlined by tiny seashells.
The hat was large enough to cover a punch bowl.
Had I noticed it before meeting her eyes, I would
have shied away from further contact with this
woman. But we were now engaged.

Who am I? Where am I going? "It's never easy
to know the answers to these questions," the woman
with the tropical hat in the dead of Minnesota winter
had said. Does she know who *she* is and where *she* is
going?

Hats worn for the purpose of making statements
brought back memories of our Bad Hair Day/No
Hair Day hats. Nancy, do you remember them as
vividly as I do?

I noticed the Hair Day hats by happenstance in
one of those countless mail-order catalogs that appear unsolicited before the holidays. I was in the
process of tossing the catalog into the recycling bin,
when it fell open to a page entitled "Hats for Every
Occasion." The page was filled with pictures of colorful baseball caps with inscriptions on their brows.
"For those bad hair days," read the caption below a
picture of a svelte model in an evening gown with
shoulder-length hair that stood on end. Above it was
a cap with the words "Bad Hair Day" inscribed in
bold letters. "For every other day" read the caption
next to a bald middle-age man resting a can of beer

against his protruding belly. Above was a cap inscribed "No Hair Day."

At that time, you'd completed only the first
couple of chemotherapy treatments. Your hair was
starting to thin out just a little, and I believe you still
held on to a vague hope that you might be one of
those rare chemotherapy patients who didn't lose all
of her hair during treatment. I hesitated ordering a
No Hair Day hat, fearing that just placing the order
might affirm a negative expectation and become self-
fulfilling. But just then you came into the kitchen
and announced that you'd lost another handful of
hair during your shower and were going out that
very afternoon to shop for turbans and wigs.

"It'll be fun! I'm going to try out some zany
hairstyles and irreverent head coverings." You'd always dressed conservatively. You still wore circle pins.
"Chemo is liberating me," you said. "From now on,
I'm Dora Dramatic!"

You made the decision for me. I ordered a pair
of Bad Hair Day/No Hair Day caps—in bright
chrome with jet-black lettering. They'd be noticeable a block away.

The hats didn't arrive for a month or so, and by
that time, you'd lost all of your hair and had a closet
full of wigs, turbans, and hats. But I noticed that
you'd not kept your "irreverence" resolve when it
came to wigs. The wigs matched your natural auburn

hair color ("strawberry blonde," you liked to say) and your short curled hairstyle almost perfectly. Only the turbans, which you wore without a wig, hinted at a bald head. As we got into bed each night your baldness was exposed. I would gently caress your scalp with my hand, discovering, with my fingertips, a part of you that I'd not known. I experienced a soft vulnerability in you that had been hidden by your hair.

"Why is the loss of hair such a big deal?" I recall asking you.

You responded by recounting the significance that women have always attached to their hair and the shame evoked by its loss. "A woman's hair is her crown," the saying goes. You hypothesized that images of being branded "unclean" and shamed by public exposure of a shaved head may even be imprinted in women at a cellular level. "The universe serves up remarkable opportunities, doesn't it," you mused. "It demands that I let go of *all* my judgments—even ones, like being branded 'unclean,' of which I was unaware until just now."

You sat up in bed and turned on the light. Your bald head was exposed for the first time to my eyes, not just my fingertips. "That's what our lives are about, isn't it! Discovering our self-imposed limitations and then discarding them. That's how we discover who we are and where we're going. What a gift!"

I sat up next to you and kissed you. First your lips. Then your soft scalp. "I know where I'm going. I'm going to love you forevermore," I said. You turned off the light. We fell back asleep.

The man in the bib overalls had placed the mannequin across one of the beach chairs. It lay face down with arms outstretched as if it had just finished the starting jump at a swimming meet. The reflection of the tropical hat hung suspended above the figure like a halo. With the Victorian table now turned on its side, the swimmer would surely collide with it upon finishing her dive. "Absurd image, isn't it?" I said to the woman next to me. "Looks like she's wearing your hat."

Nancy, I remember how your eyes lit up when I opened the box with the Bad Hair Day/No Hair Day hats. "We'll wear them to Mayo," you announced. "You wear the Bad Hair Day hat and I'll wear the No Hair Day one. I don't know that I'm prepared to wear *nothing* to cover my head. But telling it like it is. That *is* something I'm ready for."

Walking through the subterranean halls of the Mayo Clinic with our bright chrome-colored caps, heads would invariably turn. Sometimes we'd get a smile. Sometimes a "right on, sister" clenched fist. On occasion we would even be stopped by someone who wanted to know where one could get hats like ours. I noticed that our gait quickened. Everything seemed brighter and lighter. We smiled a lot.

"I feel like a celebrity," you exclaimed. "I wonder if this is what it's like for movie stars—you can't go anywhere without being noticed. It's fun, isn't it? And all it takes is telling who you are."

Of course, the people that laughed were those that resonated to lightness. They knew that life is serious—and light—both at the same time. And they knew that *taking* yourself too seriously doesn't help. It doesn't help recovery. It doesn't help the anguishing process of chemotherapy. It doesn't heal. It's extra. And, often, it hurts.

Now and then, we'd be greeted with furrowed foreheads, clenched teeth, and heads shaking from side to side. We were once accosted by a woman whose scowl was embedded in her forehead. Her cheeks were puffed and red. "It isn't funny, you know," she scolded. "My husband's chemo is killing him. You young folks just don't take *anything* seriously. Wait till one of *you* gets cancer. You'll sing a different tune."

You didn't remove the cap to reveal your bald head. "I'm so sorry for your husband," you said. "I can feel your suffering. I hope our frivolity hasn't added to it."

In retrospect, I realize that our Bad Hair Day/

No Hair Day hats constituted a public announcement of your worldview: we are here to discover who we are and where we are going; we're able to integrate it when we accept who we are without being attached to it by taking it too seriously. But Nancy, without you here, I lose sight of who I am and where I'm going. Sometimes I don't even recognize my own image reflected in a store window and strain to notice a hat that screams for attention.

"That's some hat," I said to the woman in front of the Dayton's window display. "I hope you don't take this the wrong way, but your hat looks like something that might fit right into the Caribbean display being assembled in that window. I suspect you're not wearing that hat to keep warm."

"That's exactly what I'm doing," she replied. "I'm just keeping warm. It's easy to start taking this ten-below weather too seriously. It's all a matter of attitude, you know."

I nodded to the woman. It had started to snow lightly. As I picked up my pace to get back to the office, I felt a warm gust of air from the opened door of the store. It felt almost tropical.

Nancy, I realize that neither the lady in the tropical hat nor I can change the weather. I realize you couldn't change the fact that chemo treatments made your hair fall out. I realize my love for you didn't change the course of the cancer that took your life.

But I can accept what I can't change and change
what I can—my attitude. That's what you meant,
isn't it, Nancy, by the gift of accepting who I am—
and not being attached to who I am by taking myself
too seriously.

with all my love,

Dear
Nancy,

"Serenity is more important than staying alive."

I ascribed these words to you last week in a conversation with your friend Therese. Did you actually say them, Nancy? Or did I attribute them to you because they were a statement you made in your every action, if not in your spoken words? You certainly did walk your talk, Nancy! What you may have said and what you did are starting to blend together for me.

Therese was lamenting that her daughter had refused to take her prescribed medication and, with her typical hyperbole, insisted that Lisa's health was in desperate danger. "Lisa thinks the medicine makes her gain weight and says she won't fit into her prom dress if she keeps taking the drug. How can that kid think about putting her life in jeopardy because a prom is coming up in three weeks? Is there *anything* more important than staying alive?"

Therese wanted a sympathetic ear. I gave it to her. I listened. I commiserated. She relaxed. And after the tension in her voice was gone, I responded to the question she'd asked rhetorically. I said, "Yes, there probably are things that are more important than staying alive. I think Nancy would have said that serenity is more important than staying alive."

We reminisced about occasions when you'd acted calmly while the rest of us rushed around aimlessly. About occasions on which your abiding energy took over and our rushing slowed to match your pace. About the time we were locked out of your office building before a conference and four of your associates were rushing around looking for a back door or a custodian. Paul started to jimmy the lock while I was on the cell phone calling the building manager and trying to give Paul a hand at the same time.

Serenity didn't mean that you sat around doing nothing. You also looked for solutions. But your energy was different. You arrived and calmly asked, "Why is this coming up for us? Perhaps the universe is trying to give us a message. Why would we *all* have forgotten our keys? Maybe we're not meant to be here." Of course you were right. It turned out that the conference was in a different building.

Someone said, "As you live, so you die."

That was certainly true for you, Nancy. You didn't bemoan your fate. You calmly dealt with what had to be done—waiting in doctors' offices, trying to come to terms with ambiguous test results, undergoing

numerous surgeries, becoming nauseous from chemotherapy. You seemed to know that railing against the
situation was extra—and not helpful. You'd take a
deep breath and smile in acceptance of the reception-
ist rather than demand to know why it was taking so
long to see the doctor. You said the deep breath gave
you a chance to reflect.

Therese reminded me that you often spoke on the
topic of serenity to your spiritual groups. You were
careful to point out that acceptance, which leads to
serenity, is not the same as "giving up." It's a shift in
attitude to see one's life as a cosmic game of hide-
and-seek that is unfolding for our enjoyment and
edification. "Our job is not to judge what comes up
in our lives and complain if it is not to our liking,"
you wrote in one of your essays on prayer. "Our job
is to keep asking for our truth and to stay open to
hearing the answer. Problems that present themselves
in our lives are door knockers at the gate of the
mystical dimension. The path of spiritual awakening is like a scavenger hunt: every question or problem we stumble upon is served up by God as a clue.
Problems contain the answer in hidden form as well
as the directions to the next clue. All you have to do
is open the space for the answer to become apparent
and for the next clue to be given. This requires that
we become quiet and listen. It requires adopting an

attitude of wonder instead of an attitude of judgment.
It requires serenity."

"I suppose Nancy would tell me that the answer
to the issue with Lisa's medication is somehow enfolded in the problem itself," Therese sighed. "She's
probably right. But I wish this process of going
within and searching for clues weren't so hard. I
wish the answers were written down somewhere, like
the instructions you kept in the nightstand next to
Nancy's bed."

Therese said she'd recently run across a copy of
the instructions when she was cleaning out her desk.
Nancy, you'll remember them. They're the ones
Therese and I wrote for friends who might need
guidance on what to do if an "emergency" arose.

> *To Nancy's Caregiver:*
> *Nancy believes that death is as much a*
> *part of life as living. She has no fear of dying.*
> *She is fully cognizant that her cancer is at*
> *an advanced stage. Although she continues to*
> *live every moment of this life fully and richly,*
> *she does not want to prolong this incarnation*
> *through any "heroic" or other "life saving"*
> *measures. She is at peace.*
> *You are reading this note because you think*
> *Nancy may have lost consciousness or some other*

"emergency" has happened to Nancy, which has brought into question "what should be done?" "what should I do?" or "what would Nancy want me to do?"

Most simply, the answer is "nothing." Be present to Nancy! If she is dying, be present to her dying. If she is struggling, be present to her struggling. If she is letting go, be present to her letting go. Do not try to alter the course of what is happening.

Nancy does not want to have 911 called. Nancy does not want to have paramedics try to resuscitate her. Nancy does not want to be taken to a hospital. Nancy does not want to be "saved." Please honor her desires in this regard even though they may conflict with your own desire to want to help.

Please do the following in addition to being present to her:

1. Listen to Nancy. Whatever she says goes (including countermanding all of the foregoing).

2. Please try to reach me. I also want to be present to her in the final hours of her life.

3. Communicate with the hospice staff if you need assistance.

4. Please call Julia, Mac, and my sister Dana.

Thank you.

aab

Therese and I wondered if anyone but you, she, and I had ever read the instructions. Betsy, who was with you when you died, didn't have to. There was no "emergency."

On the morning of the day you died, you told Betsy that you wanted to take a short nap before your schedule of visitors started in the afternoon. She sat by your bedside, singing lullabies until your eyes closed. You fell asleep. Betsy told me you slept soundly. So soundly that she was reminded of the times, twenty years earlier, when she'd leaned over her infant daughter's body to make sure her child was just sleeping and had not, instead, stopped breathing. Betsy nudged you, just like she'd nudged her infant daughter. But your lifeless body did not respond. Betsy remained sitting at your bedside. She didn't rush to the phone. She didn't attempt resuscitation. She sang more lullabies. This was the serenity you wanted at your side as you left this life, wasn't it, Nancy?

with all my love,

Dear
Nancy,

I'm sure I wasn't asleep. Could it have been a dream? Nancy, I'm not sure what to make of it. Let me tell you about it.

I find myself high in the mountains. This is a place I've been before. Have I hiked here? I know I've seen this view before. Or is it only parts of this view? Though real, this place seems a composite of places I've been, places we've been together. Places I've loved, places we've loved together.

I'm sitting with my legs crossed on a small, flat rock in a clearing. I look out over an open field. Beargrass in bloom. White quiet. I'm all alone. Behind me, a cirque embraces me. Though the mountains are massive and cold, the vale feels soft and comfortable. The mountain sun warms my face.

There's an expectancy about this place. It's here, in a clearing like this, looking out over the field of beargrass, that spirit guides appeared to me before in a visualization guided by your friend Giselle. An eagle once. A big brown bear. Is a guide about to appear again? My mental antennae are alert. I wait, expectantly looking over the soft white beargrass. I anticipate. Yet nothing appears.

Why do I keep being drawn to climb the mountain range behind me? I resist the call to the mountain range. The guides will eventually come, I tell myself. Just wait.

Nothing happens.

Finally, I heed my intuition. I set out for the ridge along a winding path. It's a gradual climb. Though not well traveled, the route up the mountainside is clear. Earth compacted. Rocks smoothed by hiking boots. The field of beargrass becomes more and more distant as I climb the cirque. At the top, the trail levels off to a plateau of flat granite slab above the tree line. This is desolate territory.

The plateau ends abruptly at a cliff overlooking an ocean. A clear blue expanse spreads out beyond the cliff with a shimmering calmness stretching to the horizon. The ocean is waveless, a glistening mirror reflecting the light blue sky.

"Dive," a voice says to me. "Fly."

I look out again at the sea thousands of feet below, and then, without hesitation, I let go. I have no fear. I soar from the high cliffs, gliding through the air. I need no wings. I'm carried by my own will and energy through the calm. I'm cradled in the hand of God.

The diaphanous sky merges with the waters of the ocean, and I make no splash as I enter it. I seem to unite with the ocean, barely aware that I'm swimming, not flying. Effortlessly, I slip through the water without strokes. Around me dolphins play. They dive down below the surface of the ocean, disappear, and then explode from the depths. They rise high above the ocean in a majestic arc, then crash into the still water once again. They swim, sometimes in pairs, sometimes alone, and then vanish, only to explode again suddenly into view.

A dialogue ensues with a voice within myself. "What would you like?" says the voice.

"Swim with the dolphins," I reply.

"Then swim," commands the voice.

"But how? I wouldn't be able to keep up. They're better swimmers. Can I hold on to a dolphin?"

"Ask them, not me. The dolphins will explain." The voice becomes more assertive. "Just ask. You'll be told."

I heed the voice from within. I swim, gliding effortlessly over the waveless surface, to a dolphin that seems to be waiting for me. "Hello. What can I do for you?" the dolphin asks.

"You dive down so deep. Then you explode from the depths," I respond. "I'd like to do that. But I don't have a tail to propel myself out of the water like you do."

"A tail? You think diving and exploding from the depths requires a tail? Where'd you get that idea?" The dolphin explains that they use the natural properties of the water, not their tails.

"It's easy. Go as deep as you can. The rest will take care of itself. Just be a cork. You don't have to struggle. Relax and let nature do it for you. The deeper you go, the higher you'll burst out of the water into the air. It's your own buoyancy that'll propel you from the depths into the heights."

I followed the dolphin's instructions. I swam deep. The pressure of the water increased. My eardrums and my lungs began to hurt. The pain became excruciating. I began to doubt if I'd be able to withstand the pressure of the water on my eyes. "Stay with it," said the dolphin. "The pain is just pain. It will not kill you. It is what lets you explode to great heights. You can't have one without the other."

I did as the dolphin instructed. I allowed the pain of the depths to envelop me. I didn't resist the hurt.

And then, without any effort, it all reversed. I started to come up. My own buoyancy carried me up. I exploded high into the air. What release! What freedom! Air! Space! Openness! The exhilaration of no pressure! I had moved from the depths to the heights in one continuous motion. No separate moments of pain in the depths and exhilaration in the heights. They were one.

The dolphin then turned to me. "This isn't just about playing in the ocean, dearest. It's about living. The deeper you go in experiencing your loss of me, the more exhilaration you'll feel. The more grief you allow yourself to feel for your loss of me, the more you'll open to joy. Joy and grief are one continuum. They're not separate.

"Don't resist the depths. The pressure and the pain won't kill you. The opposite. It's the buoyancy you gain from going deep into the pain that'll then allow you to experience joy—in one uninterrupted continuous motion."

The dolphin wouldn't be interrupted.

"And not just once. Not just for six months or a year. You must keep doing it. If you want joy, do it again and again. The lower you go, the higher you soar. The more you allow yourself to be crushed by the weight of the water, the more liberated you'll feel when you burst out of the water into open air. You'll learn to love the depths as much as the heights. They're one. There's no good or bad. We don't go into the depths *in order to* explode to the heights. We go to the depths because the depths and the heights are one and the same. We go to the depths to experience life fully."

"OK, OK. I get the philosophy." I had become impatient with the monologue. "But did you say I should go deep in experiencing my loss of *you*?"

The dolphin dove again, exploded into the blue sky, and, then, swam away.

with all my love,

Dear
Nancy,

Last week, Mac and I took the long way, down King's Highway past Lakewood Cemetery, to walk to my mother's house. Though mid-January, it was windbreaker weather—no hats, mittens, or scarves. Temperatures in the high thirties encouraged us to saunter. We stopped occasionally to look through the wrought-iron fence along King's Highway at the monuments in the cemetery. They were frosted white by the morning fog and glistened as they reflected the sun that was beginning to soften the frost into a glaze. We talked aimlessly—about Mac's schoolwork assignments, about his recent trip to Vail with his ski club, about his friend Charles's new girlfriend. We speculated about how you'd react to her. Mac wondered if, now that he's skiing the back bowls on his own, you'd still stand by your vow to never ski again. I mused about how different Mac's homework assignments might be now if you hadn't played such a role in pushing an inclusive academic curriculum for a student with Down syndrome. Nancy, you'd be so proud of Mac's academic accomplishments. I think he may have even surpassed your expectations. This fall he's taking mainstream Spanish, English, biology, math, and computer science.

As we came to the monument marking the graves of your mother and father, we paused. When your mother died just five years ago, it was unthinkable that you might be next. Though only your parents' markers were visible from the street, we also talked about your other relatives buried at Lakewood. I retold Mac the story of your aunt having her first husband exhumed and moved to Lakewood so that when she died, she could have her remains placed in between her first husband and her second. I expected questions from Mac about exhumation and moving dead bodies. He didn't ask any.

"Why isn't M-M-Mom here?" Mac asked. "Didn't she want her body to be buried near her family?"

Nancy, at first I didn't know quite how to respond. As long ago as I can remember, I've known you wanted to be cremated. In high school I recall sitting on a bench by Lake Harriet late at night after a date. I think we'd both just read *The Stranger* by Albert Camus for a philosophy class and were debating the true meaning of life. You identified with

Camus' sense of human isolation and were passionately arguing that each individual experience is unique.

I had started to launch into a phenomenological argument to challenge Camus' existentialism when you abruptly switched the topic. "What do you want to have done with your body when you die?" you asked. And before I could respond, you quickly added in a definitive tone of voice, "I want to be cremated."

"But why would you care?" I recall asking. "What difference could it possibly make after you're dead? If you believe in that existential stuff, it certainly can't make any difference," I reasoned. "Leave your body to science, Nancy. Have some medical student cut it up. At least that way society might get some value out of the cadaver. Camus would approve."

Seeing you were unimpressed with my argument, I did what was most comfortable—I continued with more of the same but louder. "You can't have it both ways," I harangued. "If you're attached to what happens to your body after you die, you're being completely inconsistent. No one can square attachment to the past with an existential view, in which the present experience is all that counts. As an existentialist, caring about what happens to your body just doesn't make sense."

"It doesn't matter," you sighed. You said you knew you wanted to be cremated, that's all. You didn't want to have your body decaying in the ground. You didn't want some elaborate marker. You didn't want some medical student cutting you up. You wanted to be cremated. "Andy," you pleaded softly, "promise me you'll make sure I'm cremated when I die."

"Don't you mean, 'If I die before you?'" I challenged.

In your mind, you'd moved from hypothetical conversation to making covenants. You ignored my question.

"If you die first," you vowed, "I promise I'll personally be present to make sure that *whatever* you want done with your body is done exactly the way you want. No questions asked. Make the same promise to me."

We both knew then, at seventeen, that the promise you sought to exact from me dealt with more than a hypothetical possibility. Though I don't think we'd ever said it out loud, we both knew in our hearts that we'd go off to college in different states, that even though we'd date others, there'd never be anyone else for either of us, and that during graduate school, we'd be married and live together until one of us died. Unless we were both hit by the same truck, one of us would necessarily end up acting on the vows you wanted us to exchange that very night.

"Promise me," you pleaded.

I did promise. More than thirty years ago I made a promise to you that I would attend to the cremation of your body. I implicitly renewed that promise again every decade or so when you revised the instructions you left in my desk drawer about what was to be done at your memorial service. In those instructions, the hymns periodically changed. The readings changed. Who would officiate changed. But your being cremated, that never changed.

Mac tugged at my sleeve. I'd still not responded to his question about why your body hadn't been buried alongside the rest of your family.

"I don't know, Mac," I finally replied. "Mom told me she wanted to be cremated and didn't want a fancy marker."

"Wh-wh-why?" he persisted.

I responded by saying that the essential things in life are often ones for which you have no reason. That the important thing is to make your wishes known, so that others aren't burdened with having to make a decision for you and guess about what you might have wanted.

"You know, Mac, every one of us will someday be a corpse. Have you thought about what you'd want done with your body?" I asked.

"I want to be with Mom," Mac replied. "I know she's in my heart. But I want to see her face."

As we rounded the corner at 36th Street, I noticed that the gates to the cemetery were open. We entered and followed the driveway around to the chapel.

Nancy, as you know, the chapel at Lakewood is built on the hillside overlooking the cemetery. However, you may not know that directly below the chapel's delicately arched dome, with its inlaid mosaic tile, lies the working part of a crematorium—the cremation retort. The entrance to the retort is on the backside of the hill, hidden from the entrance to the chapel. There, the softness of the chapel is juxtaposed to the functionality of a retort, built to withstand temperatures exceeding 1,700 degrees Fahrenheit. Massive metal doors open into the side of the hill to provide access to the crematorium. From this side of the hill, you enter a cave, not a chapel.

Mac and I found ourselves at the closed entrance to the cave. We'd been here before—just six months ago, on the third day after you died. On that afternoon, Jim, Chad, and I had lifted your body from the bed in which you died, laid it in the casket Chad and I had helped build, and carried the casket into the cave's gaping mouth.

The retort's cast-iron doors are set in slabs of gray Minnesota granite. Like prison doors, they leave no

doubt that they're meant to definitively separate this
world from a different one. Your simple casket appeared overwhelmed by the massiveness of the stone
and cast iron. We slowly edged the casket forward
into the opening. For a while, it rested there, one
end supported by the lip of the retort and the other
by Chad, Julia, Mac, and me. You had asked me to
be present, Nancy. I was present. I kept the promises
I made to you in high school, sitting on a bench by
Lake Harriet.

Though the inner door to the retort was closed,
the dry heat of the crematorium furnaces appeared
to overpower the humidity of the hot July afternoon.
We were in the bowels of a mechanism designed to
eradicate all animate matter. It did not, however,
eradicate anima. We sang your favorite hymns and
spirituals: "Swing Low, Sweet Chariot"; "Shall We
Gather at the River?" We cried. I spoke. I spoke
about how much I appreciated you. I spoke of my
gratitude for your being my wife, my lover, my friend,
the mother of my children, my guide. But I did not
mention the promise I'd made to you when we were
seventeen. Instead, I just made sure that it was my
hand that was the last one to touch the casket as it
disappeared into the retort.

"Nancy, I love you," I whispered. The doors
closed shut. The casket was consumed.

Mac and I had been standing in the shade of

the entrance to the crematorium long enough to begin to feel the cold of even a mild January day in Minnesota. "Let's move into the sunshine and warm up, Mac. Do you remember how hot it was when we were here last?" I asked. "I feel like I still experience the sensation of that heat on my skin. It's left a permanent mark on me."

"M-m-me too," replied Mac.

We turned and again headed toward my mother's house. As we began to walk, a rainbow appeared in the sky. In mid-January. In Minnesota. A full rainbow!

"Mac, look!" I exclaimed. "A rainbow in January. That's incredible!"

"Mom's marker," Mac replied authoritatively.

with all my love,

Dear
   Nancy,

"I guess that's what happens when you turn fifty," you said, raising your eyebrows and pursing your lips. "Just one lousy week without jogging around Lake Harriet every day, and I'm already out of shape. I was winded before I ran half the lake and ended up walking home from just beyond the bandstand. Why does staying in shape have to be so hard?"

A week later, you were breathless before reaching the fishing dock at Russell Avenue. Then before reaching Minnehaha Parkway. No coughing. No fever. No bleeding. No chest pain. Just shortness of breath.

Two weeks later, when you made an appointment to see your doctor, we still didn't acknowledge that shortness of breath could presage something serious. Shortness of breath was an inconvenience, not a disability. Not enough to merit serious attention.

Stage-four ovarian cancer metastasized to the

lungs, now *that* was serious. Suddenly we were forced to pay attention.

We paid attention to more than a diagnosis that left us stunned. We began paying attention to the life-giving essence itself, breath.

From the day of the diagnosis until the day of your death, I observed you breathe thousands of breaths. Deep, relaxed breaths. Short, gasping breaths. Breaths that you breathed on your own and breaths that were breathed for you by a ventilator in an intensive-care room. Breaths you breathed when you were awake. Breaths that you breathed while you were asleep.

Occasionally, I'd intentionally synchronize my in-breath with your in-breath. Your out-breath with my out-breath. I'd feel as if we'd become one unified breathing organism. Cool outside air entered my lungs, your belly rose. Warm air left my body through my nostrils, your chest fell.

The more time I spent with you in the simple act of breathing, the less clarity I had about what was really happening. I'm beginning to conclude, Nancy, that you and I were *being breathed*. It's as if the universe were an immense ventilator. It fills our lungs and lifts our chests autonomically. It dictates the rhythm of our inhalations and exhalations, all without any action on our part. We are beach toys being inflated and deflated by some unseen bellows.

You liked to remind me that the word in Hebrew for breath, *ruach,* is the same as the word for wind and for spirit. Nancy, I've come to see that *ruach* is more than just a metaphor for a connection between the material and the nonmaterial worlds. I've come to see that breathing imbues us with spirit—and that we *are* spirit.

I recall sitting next to you, holding your hand, attending to your breath after one of your surgeries. "My whole body feels bruised, like I'd been dropped from the gurney," you said. "But your touch and the merging of your breath with mine has changed all that. I feel I've recovered my connection to the source."

And you had. Dr. Wilson remarked that he'd never seen a patient fully recover from a radical pleurodeisis in just forty-eight hours and leave the hospital.

We were soon outdoors walking once again around your beloved Lake Harriet. The zephyrs coming across the lake touched more than our cheeks. They became a conscious part of an in-breath and an out-breath. Crystal clear. Crisp. The cold Minnesota air was *ruach.*

When Julia's in town, the three of us take the same route around Lake Harriet that you did. Last week, as we passed the bandstand, Mac said he felt you in the wind. Julia abruptly stopped and demanded Mac's full attention. "What do you mean, Mac? I bet this place just *reminds* you of Mom."

"Nope," he replied. "She's *in* the wind. I hear her v-v-voice."

Julia and Mac stopped walking. "What are Mom's exact words, Mac?" Julia demanded. "Do you hear her voice in your ear or in your heart?"

"She talks in my ear and in my heart."

"Oh, yeah? How does she do that?"

"Just be quiet and listen. B-breathe the wind. Mind the wind. Pay attention to the breath inside your body. Then you will hear her."

Julia resumed walking. Goose bumps rippled across the water. The gust had the beginning of a fall crispness. We picked up an exercise pace.

"Mom says to me she's here right now." Mac was hurrying to keep up with Julia's pace. "She touches my cheek with her hand. Mom's words comfort me."

Wind. Breath. Spirit. *Ruach.*

Are they really just Hebraic linguistics, Nancy?

with all my love,

Dear
Nancy,

Yesterday, I spent the entire morning rummaging through your jewelry drawers, hoping to find a gift for Julia's birthday. The theme for this birthday—her twenty-first—was to be Julia's roots. I wanted to give Julia two pieces of jewelry, one that symbolized your French Huguenot roots and another that symbolized my roots in Latvia.

Do you remember the large amber brooch my mother gave you on your thirtieth birthday? Although a bit too formal, I thought that because it is inescapably ethnic, it would make an ideal present for Julia on this significant day. Not only is it made of amber, a typically Latvian stone, the brooch has been in my family for three generations. I admit that the pin is not really Julia's style. I doubt she'll ever wear it. But I hoped she would cherish it anyway as a symbol of her heritage.

I was less sure of what item of jewelry would be right to symbolize Julia's heritage from you, Nancy. Julia already has a number of pieces connected to

your French Huguenot roots. At sixteen, your
mother gave Julia your great-grandmother's ruby
ring. Then, after your mother died, Julia ended
up with your mother's antique hairpin.

A month or so after you died, your sister Marge
asked me if she could have the sapphire bracelet that
you had inherited from your mother. I felt Marge
had more of a rightful claim to it than I did, and
bargaining about sapphire bracelets seemed so insig-
nificant, even disrespectful to you. I could only think
about how much I loved you and missed you. I gave
it to Marge without thinking about Julia. But now,
with your mother's bracelet gone, I realized that
there isn't any significant jewelry left with historical
ties to your family.

I decided instead to give Julia something that
represented your essence, not your roots. For me, the
choice was simple: the gold pendant in the shape of
an open hand with a heart in the middle of it. I had
given it to you on our twentieth wedding anniversary.
An opened hand and a heart were so perfectly *you*—
loving, giving, and accepting, all at the same time.
You wore the necklace most every day. It would make
a perfect present for Julia on this special occasion.

I opened your jewelry boxes one by one, searching for the gold necklace. Nancy, was there any logic
to the way you organized your jewelry? A pearl necklace in the same box with costume jewelry. Circle

pins together with earrings. My favorites, which you wore regularly, were there lying next to items of jewelry I don't recall ever seeing on you. Was I not paying sufficient attention, or did you wear my favorites so often that the rest became a blur?

A lifetime of events were impregnated in your jewelry. I was flooded with memories. The black pearls went with the low-cut, long black velvet dress that you would wear on formal occasions. The diamond earrings went with the short green outfit that you wore dancing. I sorted through jewelry that you wore only on holidays—holly branch and mistletoe pins at Christmas, large dangling orange earrings around Thanksgiving. I discovered jewelry that I don't remember seeing on you since we were in college.

But the heart with the open hand pendant was nowhere to be found. I even looked in the hidden drawer in your vanity where you kept jewelry too valuable to keep exposed. I couldn't find it anywhere.

Where could you have put it? I wondered. You would not have put it in the safe deposit box. Did you have another spot for storing jewelry other than your dressing room? I began searching desperately through drawers that I knew were not even a remote possibility.

In the middle of lifting through your nightgowns, I suddenly realized what had happened. The necklace had been cremated with your body. How

could I have forgotten? We intentionally placed the
things that were most precious to you with your
body when it was moved from our bed and placed
into the casket for cremation. The afghan from Marge
covered your legs. The teddy bear Mac had given you
when you were sick with pneumonia ten years ago
was at your feet. The polar bear that Betsy gave you
was at your side. The vase with the ostrich feather;
the framed photograph of the Yazzie sculpture—
things you never failed to take with you to a hospital room—were admired for a last time and gently
placed in the casket next to your body. Therese put
her earrings in. The casket became filled with things
you loved from people who loved you.

I closed my eyes and in a flash I could remember
lifting your body from our bed, the pendant hang-
ing from the neck of your body as it always had.
The delicate chain curled along the neckline, nestled
along the outside of the clavicle, outlining the collar-
bone with serpentine grace. The pendant lay nestled
erotically between your breasts, the buttons to your
nightgown concealing part of it.

I had been flooded with conflicting thoughts
and emotions. In less than a split second my mind
raced through a crazy internal dialogue. How could
I be noticing the outline of your breasts against your
nightgown at a time like this? If rigor mortis has set
in, has the pendant somehow become glued to the

body? Can it be removed without doing damage and without destroying the sanctity of this moment? Yet, this is a piece of jewelry valued more for its memories than for any monetary amount; I can't just let it be disintegrated. But if I try to remove it, what will people think? "That cheapskate," I could hear them saying to themselves.

The thought of removing the necklace without anyone noticing flashed through my mind as I envisioned myself performing a Houdiniesque sleight of hand while your body was being moved from bed to coffin. But I knew the clasp was difficult to maneuver. I knew that I did not have the courage to be embarrassed by groping and fumbling around while people looked on. Why had I not planned in advance? Why had I not focused on the necklace, and what would happen to it? Why had I not paid more attention as I lay next to your body? Perhaps I had made a mistake after all in not having a mortuary service involved. They would have attended to the mechanics of removing jewelry and preparing the body discreetly, outside of the presence of family and friends.

On reflection, I doubt that I would have done anything differently had I thought about it before we moved your body. The necklace was meant not to be removed from your body. Your wedding band was meant not to be removed from your body. These material symbols of nonmaterial aspects of you were meant to stay with your body and become indistinguishable from the remains of your flesh—part of the dust that would be scattered in a few days at our wilderness retreat.

Yet on occasion I yearn for the material. My fingers long to feel the shape of the heart inside the hand with its outstretched fingers. My eyes long to see the glint of light reflected from the pendant. Part of me yearns for this tangible metaphor for your being a person with an open heart and a giving hand. It is the same part of me that still yearns for the touch of your skin, and remembers the texture of your hair. Are your skin and hair, like the pendant, just symbols of nonphysical aspects of you? Does clinging to those physical aspects block my experience of the essence that they symbolize? Do I let these physical aspects develop into a brick wall that obstructs my vision of that essence?

In my support group for grieving spouses, I learned that nearly half of the members of the group disposed of the decedent's clothing immediately. Some were counseled by friends and family that having closets full of clothes would bring up painful memories. Others were told that the clothes would interfere with the healthy goal of "getting on" with their lives. Members of the group that hadn't cleaned out closets right away, cherished having the clothes around. They are soft, gentle relics, they said. The touch of the clothes is familiar. The aromas are still potent. Some said they take the clothes out, just to feel them and smell them. One of the women in my group said that when her skin hungers for her deceased husband's physical touch, nothing comforts her more than wearing his oldest moth-eaten sweater.

Though your closets are still filled with your clothes, I've not connected to you through them. Julia occasionally looks through your wardrobe and finds something that she'd like to wear. Mac, too, digs out your sweatpants on rainy afternoons and, after lounging on the couch in your study, hides them again in the back corner of his dresser drawer—so that they won't be washed, I suspect. What will Mac do when they wear out? Like everything else, Nancy, your sweatpants are impermanent.

I suppose impermanence is the reason why the heart-with-the-open-hand pendant had to be cremated. I would have clung to that little piece of gold just a bit too much. It would have been too perfect an icon to represent your essence. I'd have been devastated if it were lost and would have experienced again the anxiety I felt searching for it as a gift for Julia. It would have become yet another loss to be grieved.

For Julia's birthday, I decided to give her something transitory: a trip to visit our ancestral homes in Latvia and the Loire Valley. Nancy, will you be our guide?

with all my love,

Dear
Nancy,

About a month before you died, we were driving back to Minneapolis from the Mayo Clinic, and you announced that you'd decided not to undergo further chemotherapy.

"What?" The bumper-to-bumper traffic on Highway 52 as it merges with Highway 55 kept me from doing more than quickly turning my head to see if your facial expression mirrored the gravity of your words. "You're not talking about giving up, are you?"

"No, I'm more positive than ever," you replied. "But until Dr. Wilson explained this morning that sisplatinum wasn't doing the job, I hadn't really allowed myself to fully accept this disease as *mine*. I think I harbored the belief that something external was capable of eradicating the cancer."

I changed lanes and slowed to ten miles under the speed limit instead of ten miles over. I could now focus my peripheral vision on you instead of the highway patrol car I'd been nervously anticipating.

"What's changed is that I'm no longer in a battle," you continued. "I feel like I've finally relaxed into allowing the natural course of events to unfold. I've realized that this disease isn't my enemy."

You reasoned that we're all on a path of dying. That healing doesn't mean that you stop being on that path. "I may heal unto life. Or I may heal unto death," you reflected. "But if I'm going to heal, it's because I've accepted death, not because I've fought it."

Somehow, your words seemed to make perfect sense to me then, and since so many of our friends depended on the "hotline"—my day-to-day voice mail updates on your condition—we agreed that I needed to say something on the hotline about the shift in your perspective. All I intended to do was describe what I thought was a subtle change. The distinction between a path of healing—with the acknowledged possibility of death, and the path of dying—with the expectation of recovery, was, in my mind, mostly poetic.

When we got home, I dictated a message for the hotline. Though you listened to it before I put it on the answering machine, I don't recall that we discussed the specific words. But acknowledging your shift in attitude must have been quite a milestone. I've no recollection of what went through my mind at the time. Recently, I've been wondering what let me feel comfortable publicly broadcasting a statement about your being on a "path of dying" even if it was tempered by a statement that you had an "expectation of recovery." I wish I still had the message. Perhaps the words might shed some light on what shift there might have been in *my* perspective.

Last week, I was wondering out loud to your friend Therese about the message, trying to remember the precise words I had used. To my surprise, she told me that your friend Margaret had tape-recorded some of the messages. She suggested I call Margaret to ask if she still had the transcripts.

Margaret said she'd taped quite a few of the hotline updates. They were a remarkable gift, she said. Your friends depended on them. The messages described not only your physical condition but your mental and spiritual state as well. So the hotline freed your friends to talk to you at a deeper level. It gave them the ability, for example, to talk to you about the meaning of friendship and the meaning of life. To talk about the meaning of suffering in general. She said your friends felt relieved to know that you were not burdened by having to repeat the same information dozens of times in response to the obvious questions about what a doctor said or what the test results showed.

But Margaret also pointed out that the hotline eliminated the normal conversation starters. Deprived of superficial chatter as a way to "break the ice," your friends were forced to go deeper right away.

Margaret said she had liked to talk to you about books that had an impact on her spiritual life. Her favorite lines of poetry. Picking out something that was meaningful enough to read to her closest friend, knowing it might be the very last thing she'd ever read to you. That, Margaret said, was a challenge. The last time she came to visit you, she said she'd spent days going through her library to find the right passage.

"Why is it that we don't give the same degree of thoughtfulness to things that we say?" Margaret asked me. "Rationally, I should have been much more concerned about what I *said* than something I selected to *read*."

She mused that without the hotline, her last words to you might well have been about your physical condition, and she might well have told you some anecdote about someone who'd been cured by shark's fin. Instead, at her last visit with you, she'd read you Rachel Remen's poem "Mother Knows Best":

> *Don't talk about your trouble*
> *No one loves a sad face*
> *Oh Mom, the truth is*
> *Cheer isolates*
> *Competence intimidates*

> *Control separates*
> *and sadness*
> *Sadness opens us each to the other.*

"Even now I have a hard time reciting the poem without choking up a bit," Margaret said to me. "But, of course, the readings always ended up just being a springboard for deeper dialogue." On that visit, you and she didn't talk much about the poem. You talked about your own neediness. You talked about how suffering rips away masks. You'd told her that, with cancer, you felt you'd joined the class of the afflicted for the first time. "Affliction is a powerful teacher," Margaret quoted you. She said your words have stayed with her to this day.

It turned out that Margaret hadn't tape-recorded the hotline update for which I was looking. "Oh well," I sighed. "I'd hoped to get some insight into what was going through my mind when I announced that Nancy considered herself to be on a 'path of dying.'" For, in spite of the fact that you and I talked about death frequently, and in spite of the fact that I was with you during each chemotherapy and surgery and listened with you to every doctor's report, I still never believed that your dying was a real possibility.

"The words don't matter," replied Margaret. "That's why the hotline was such a blessing for us.

It got the words out of the way. It let us communicate without words."

As I left, Margaret and I bowed to each other.
Words had become unnecessary.

with all my love,

SELF-TRANSFORMATION

from *Gifts of Spirit;* spirituality lecture series,
March 1991

. . . Our real job as Christians is not to convert others but to transform ourselves. As each of us finds peace in our heart (and we must be actively involved in this, as healing cannot be accomplished without our participation), we begin to radiate a light that warms and heals everyone we contact. We transform the world by being. We don't have to do something. Finding one's true self changes the world. In fact, wanting to reform the world without discovering one's true self is like trying to cover the world with leather to avoid the pain of walking on stones and thorns. It is much simpler to wear shoes.

*Dear
Nancy,*

Driving home from our wilderness retreat yesterday, the skies put on a spectacular azure blue, iridescent fete. Diaphanous clouds. The burning white sphere of the sun gradually turned red, lighting the clouds in a warming hearth. And then, the sphere sank into nothingness, turning the crystalline skies to cobalt.

"Did you notice the color of the sky?" I asked Mac, who was blasting *Grease* on his Walkman and rocking back and forth to the lyrics he's heard a hundred times. "The sky's such a familiar blue."

Mac was in the process of doing permanent damage to his eardrums. He didn't hear me. I didn't push but made a hand gesture for turning down the volume on the tape player.

"Yeah. What?" Mac asked when the song had finished and he'd detached himself from the earphones. "What do you w-want, Dad?"

"I was noticing the color of the sky," I said. "I was mesmerized by it. I don't think I've ever seen a sky quite this color before, yet it seems like I've known it all my life. Did you notice how light the blue was without being flat? The color appeared three-dimensional."

"It's the color of Mom's eyes." Mac's response was matter-of-fact. "The sky changes just like Mom's eyes change when it gets dark. Her spirit's in the sky winking." Mac returned to his music. He's not mystified by the ineffable.

I suppose you would, indeed, have winked at me this weekend. I'm having to learn to be a host, and I struggle to do the things that you appeared to do so effortlessly: suggesting activities for our guests; organizing games for the young people, walks for the older; serving meals to large groups; letting guests participate in selected chores so they feel useful but not overburdened; "letting go" when things don't get done exactly as I would have liked them. Nancy, I've learned it is not effortless. I stub my toe often. I feel awkward, and I miss you.

What's hardest for me is to stop the running of the tapes of unfinished things-to-do in my mind. Before you died, it seemed that activities that absorbed my complete attention were possible: I'd check the thermometer, roll some snow between my fingers, select a wax for my cross-country skis, and head off to the Birkie trail.

At the fish hatchery, where I usually start my prac-

tice loop, the trail disappears into the woods. I'd be
in complete solitude. The hum of the skis gliding effortlessly on the fresh snow would be complemented
by the crunch of the poles biting through the surface
of the snow. My upper body would relax onto the
poles. I'd recall my coach's imagery of the skier's
body as the arm on the pump of an oil derrick. My
body's weight would collapse forward, dynamically
off balance, I'd catch a glimpse of the reminder notes
I've written in black marker on the tips of my skis:
high hip; loose arm; have fun. I'd experience my position on the skis, the position of the skis on the snow,
the rhythm of pole plant as the terrain changes from
flat to hilly. Nothing extraneous. I'd drink in the
crisp coldness of the air. I'd glide as if flying. No
part of me would be at home, thinking of guests or
the next meal.

Not so now. Last weekend, I didn't glide effortlessly on the Birkie trail. I wasn't dynamically off
balance. I was just off. My mind was back at the
house, not on the sharp turn or the fast drop at the
forty-two-kilometer mark. I struggled with plans for
the evening while I struggled against the skis. Would
Mac be OK alone with Wayne? Could I get away with
serving pasta again? I now realize that hosting is different than entertaining.

I've also learned that mothering is different than
fathering. You were right in what you said to me

about Mac: he needs loving. What you didn't say, but I guess I should have inferred, is that he needs the kind of loving *you* gave him: just being with him without doing anything special. Mothering.

A couple of weeks ago, Mac had an English homework assignment in which he had to match vocabulary words with their definitions. It was a simple worksheet that Mrs. Havner uses to build vocabulary in the remedial reading class. By the time Mac came to see me for help, he'd already drawn lines connecting the same vocabulary word to boxes around three unrelated definitions.

I made no attempt to determine from Mac what magical connection he'd found among the definitions. Instead, I lectured him about mutually exclusive propositions, belaboring principles of Aristotelian logic without any appreciation that I was talking to a boy with Down syndrome. At the end of my monologue, Mac announced that you, Nancy, were the only one who understood him. I know Mac meant both that you clearly heard his often unintelligible words and, as well, that you knew who he is and what he needs in order to be understood. *Understand*— yet another word with multiple definitions?

I have a new appreciation for a non-dictionary meaning of the word *understand*. You *stood under* Mac. You supported him. Your loving kindness underpinned him. I think Mac knows that I don't yet under-stand him the way you did. But I'm learn-ing. Slowly.

Earlier this week, Mac complained of being sick. A slight fever—just under 100. Body aches. A little headache, but no stomachache. My first inclination was to encourage him to "tough it out" by going to school and suggesting that he call me at work from school if things got worse. But I know Mac loves school and isn't looking for excuses to malin-ger. He said he wanted to stay home in bed. I didn't have anything at the office that I couldn't handle from home. I let him stay in bed.

I made Mac breakfast, served him in bed, and read a couple of chapters of his new *Goosebumps* book out loud to him. I listened to him tell me about his aches without immediately trying to find a way to fix the aches, or him. I winked to let him know I'd under-stood his soul, not just his words. I moved slowly. By the end of the day, Mac's aches had disappeared. His headache was gone. He had no fever. Nancy, I'm be-ginning to under-stand.

Mac is right: your spirit was winking through the azure blue skies on the drive home last weekend, wasn't it? You knew I'd struggled. You knew I needed a sign of your spirit's presence—the presence that's helped me learn mothering.

But I also long for your touch, Nancy. I long for your hand on my shoulder that goes with your wink. I yearn for more than spirit.

I recall the conference we attended with the Dalai Lama years ago. Someone from the audience asked the Dalai Lama to distinguish between spirit and soul. He remarked that he experiences spirit as the high places—the skies and the light—and soul as the low places—the valleys and the deep rivers.

Nancy, it's the low places I miss so much right now. My soul is empty without you. Though the skies are spectacular, I yearn for the valleys and the deep rivers. Where are they? Where are you?

with all my love,

*Dear
Nancy,*

Just a week or two after you died, an advertisement in the summer issue of *The Turning Wheel* caught my eye:

> *Zen Hospice Project*
> *Training for practitioners in Zen Hospice work*
> *Two-week classroom training*
> *Positions for hospice work available*

I ripped the page from the magazine and dialed the telephone number at the bottom of the advertisement. It was Saturday. I half-expected to talk to an answering machine. But my call was answered by an intake interviewer.

"I'm not a Buddhist," I stammered. "I don't practice Zen. But I feel called to be involved in being present to the dying." I asked the intake interviewer to send me an application, and I gave him my fax number.

The intake interviewer didn't ask me to spell my

name or to repeat the fax number. "Tell me about *yourself*," he said. "What interests you in this work?"

I explained that I'd been together with you for the year before you died in a state of attentiveness that I could only describe as "Zen-like." I experienced each moment—even those moments when I was changing rancid, ooze-filled bandages—without judging the experience as "good" or "bad." I felt I'd acknowledged what was presenting itself moment to moment with loving acceptance. I wanted to continue being present to others in that manner.

The intake interviewer seemed unimpressed by the importance I attached to mindful attention. He appeared unmoved by my description of the richness of my experience with you. "Tell me more," he said.

"And I want to be of service." I reasoned that the program would be looking for people that could staff a hospice facility in San Francisco. That there would be little benefit for them to train someone from Minneapolis. That I'd have to persuade the intake interviewer of my altruistic motivations. "I've been thinking about helping out in a nursing home. But I've noticed that caregivers often approach dying from a stance of pity. I was hoping a Zen approach would bring freedom from such value judgments. I want to make a difference."

There was no immediate response, and I'm embarrassed to admit, Nancy, that I took advantage of the silence to "casually" mention that I sit on the board of directors of a large medical clinic. The interviewer was equally unaffected by my credentials.

"Do you think you're emotionally prepared for this kind of work?" he asked.

How dare this person question whether I'm adequately suited, I thought. After all, what we're talking about here is just a *volunteer* position. I felt the project should be grateful that someone with *my* background would even be interested.

"How long ago did your wife die?" the interviewer continued.

My thinking moved from questioning to judging. This is no Zen Buddhist, I decreed. He's a Westerner, limited to seeing reality solely in the context of linear time. Are the number of twenty-four-hour days that have elapsed since a death relevant to the presence one brings to life? Impatiently, I responded that though we'd cremated a part of you just two weeks ago, other parts of you had died decades ago. Still others continue to live as we speak.

"We generally don't accept applicants unless their motivations are absolutely clear." The intake interviewer's tone was matter-of-fact. "With such a major loss occurring so recently, it must be hard to be clear about *anything*—much less your motivations for taking on something as intense as this." The intake interviewer asked if I'd mind his talking candidly to me about grief.

I sensed a lecture was coming. One was.

With a death, there's often incomplete business, the intake interviewer explained. There needs to be closure. Sometimes, the survivor isn't consciously aware for months, sometimes even for years, of issues that need closure.

"After losing your wife of—did you say thirty?—years, we'd expect you to experience shock, denial, and despair—just to mention a few of the countless emotions that are a part of grief. These are intense emotions. They'll take you on a roller-coaster ride. These feelings may surprise and overwhelm you when you'd least expect them to."

The lecture continued. The intake interviewer said that hospice work is about being present to the process of the *dying* person. And that Zen practice is about clarity. A dying person would likely be experiencing guilt, loss and fear around *his* or *her* death—the same feelings I'm still likely to be experiencing around *your* death. With your having died just weeks earlier, my *own* grief process would likely begin to mingle with the dying person's process—not conducive to clarity for me or for the dying person. The interviewer said he'd be concerned that, at this point, it would be hard for me to know if I'm working out my own feelings—rather than being fully present to the feelings of the person who's dying.

"I appreciate your desire to give back," the interviewer concluded. "But even feelings of wanting to give back can interfere with the process of dying with clarity. Give your grief dignity. Let it take its course."

I protested. I argued that my process with you *was* complete and that we had no unfinished business. I argued that I did have clarity. That neither of us hid from the reality of what was happening and that I could be present to others without having my emotions interfere. I tried to persuade the interviewer that I was an exception to their general rule.

"In unusual cases, we may make an exception," conceded the interviewer. He said that in extraordinary cases the training program might consider admitting an applicant as early as six or seven months following a major loss. But that doesn't happen often. Usually a training program of this kind isn't appropriate for at least a year after a major loss, he said. "Call us back next summer. We're planning to offer another session next year. Perhaps then." The intake interviewer paused.

"*If* you're still interested," he added.

It turned out that the next training session was scheduled just six months after the one I'd been so desperate to attend—not almost a year later, as the interviewer had assumed when we'd talked. But I read the new ad in the winter issue of *The Turning Wheel* without picking up the phone to register, without even clipping the ad for future reference.

Instead, I sighed. My anger at the intake interviewer's cross-examination should have been a signal to me that I was far from ready to make any significant decisions. The interviewer had been right. Not enough time had passed. My interest in the Zen hospice project had, indeed, been motivated by incomplete feelings around your death, not passion to be present to the dying process of someone else. I was clinging to memories of you and wanted to live again our last twelve months together. And I now realize that I was unconsciously prepared to have someone else be a surrogate for my memories. I did need time to grieve.

Yet there is more. More has occurred than the mere *passage* of time. The *quality* of time has changed.

In one of your adult education talks at church, I remember you speaking of the distinction between *kyros*—time as experienced—and *chronos*—time according to the clock. You said that perceptions of time change when one experiences something fully and is completely present. Sometimes such experiences are called "altered" states of consciousness.

During the last year of your life, we were living *kyros,* weren't we, Nancy. The facts were these: You

were sick. You might die. I knew I would hold your
hand during every moment of the journey, living together whatever was unfolding. Both of us saw each
step in that journey as an opportunity to appreciate
the magical uniqueness of each moment and each
other. You said to me that the year after your diagnosis was one of the best years of your life, not one
of the worst. You said you experienced a lifetime of
love. Time had slowed down. We were in a state of
altered consciousness.

Nancy, I now realize that over the past six months
"real" time—*chronos*—again predominates. In the
past six months, 180 days of *chronos* have elapsed. But
in the same 180 days, a lifetime of *kyros* has passed.
I now see that I needed not only a year of *chronos* in
order to let grief take its course, as the intake interviewer suggested, but time to allow my state of consciousness to adapt to loving you without being able
to see you.

with all my love,

*Dear
Nancy,*

Yesterday I had lunch with Al Lourd. Al retired about three or four years ago. He'd been traveling and just recently learned of your death. He called
to express his condolences. "Did you know my wife,
Diane, also died of ovarian cancer?" Al asked.

I didn't. Our paths had crossed only to work on
corporate finance transactions. I knew every nuance
of his company's income statement. But I didn't even
know for sure that he was married. We made arrangements to get together for lunch at the Minneapolis
Club.

I felt out of place. The Minneapolis Club is a business milieu. We'd come here to discuss death, not to
make deals. But Al put me at ease. He hadn't wanted
to be interrupted in the main dining room by feeling
the need to greet members of his old lunch group.
He'd made reservations in back, in the Crystal Room.

We began by sharing our experiences of the
road trip from Minneapolis to the Mayo Clinic
in Rochester. We reflected on the intimacy of our

respective conversations during the eighty-mile drive there, on the loneliness of the trips back on the occasions when you or Diane stayed in Rochester overnight and we returned to the Twin Cities to work.

Trips back were usually late at night. Highway 52 would be empty except for semitrailers appearing out of the darkness like giant refrigerators on wheels. The fields of farmland became a horizonless sea. Broken only occasionally by the red neon of an all-night gas station. Often, it would begin to snow. The flat, white pavement would become an extension of hospital bed sheets.

About halfway back to the Twin Cities, the chemical processing plant in Rosemont would appear on the horizon. Its smokestacks and silos would be dotted with bright white Christmas tree lights—a fairyland city appearing out of the sea. Oz. Then, as we'd near Oz, smoke billowing from the smokestacks would reflect from lit silos, creating an eerie backdrop for the red flames shooting skyward. Even with the windows closed, acrid fumes would penetrate the car.

This is no Oz, we'd realize. The glimmering in the distance was industrial pollution, not fairy dust. The magic would vanish. We'd be back in town.

Al told me that Diane had a history of cancer in her family, and she saw her gynecologist regularly. Although she had no symptoms, she decided to have

a hysterectomy performed as a prophylactic measure. During the surgery, it was discovered that she
had a sizable tumor and was told that she had only
a couple of years—at best. She died almost exactly
two years later.

"I don't think I ever believed that Nancy's dying
was really a possibility," I said. "I'm not sure what
thoughts would have been going through my head
on those trips back from Rochester if I'd thought
death was a meaningful possibility."

"You weren't told?" Al's bushy eyebrows almost
reached his hairline. "At Mayo? With their 'team' approach? We never held out any hope that treatments
would result in a cure. The chemo and the surgeries
were just a way to give us the full two years that we
were promised."

No one ever did say to us, did they, that you had
two years, or two months, or two weeks to live? Were
we told and unwilling to let it in? You looked good.
You were full of energy. Just three weeks before you
died, you scheduled a trip to Kentucky to visit your
brother. You decided not to go, not because you were
infirm, but because you wanted to spend the weekend
at our wilderness retreat in Wisconsin.

If we had been told, would we have been in-
capable of hearing because we were certain that healing was only partly physical? Had our experience

with my meningitis fifteen years ago—when I *had* been told that I had a life expectancy of two years *at best*—deluded us? I'm still alive. You would also live, we must have reasoned subconsciously.

You would find meaning in the disease and live, we must have concluded. You would discover the energy that had been blocked in your body and manifested itself as ovarian cancer. You would come to understand its symbolism and dissolve the blockage. Your *chi* would begin to circulate freely again. The surgeries and chemotherapies would be springboards to launch you into self-exploration that would constitute your true healing. We were on a path of self-realization. The disease was a teaching on that path. Why did it never occur to me that death itself might be on the path of self-realization?

We *had* been told that you had stage-four ovarian cancer. We knew that stage four was geometrically more serious than stage two or stage three. Yet, the numbers were abstractions. The probabilities were statistics. They did not apply to you.

As I sat with Al, I began to wonder if we would have lived the last year of your life differently if your dying had been stated as a certainty, like it had for Al and Diane. Would we have made fewer trips to Rochester? Would we have read more books together? Would we have taken more trips to visit Julia

in Boston and fewer trips to Santa Fe or Oak Creek
Canyon? Would we have spent more time at Ghost
Ranch, walking in the red rock?

I remember your saying to me, "Andy, I feel my
chi returning. But if I'm wrong, if I should die, I
want you to know that these have been the best
months of my life. The best *ever*. It hasn't been
easy. Sometimes the pain's been unbearable. But
I wouldn't trade these months for *anything*."

You handed me a copy of a book open to a poem
by Wu-Men, written in the twelfth century:

> *Ten thousand flowers in spring,*
> *the moon in autumn*
> *A cool breeze in summer,*
> *snow in winter—*
> *If your mind is not clouded*
> *by unnecessary things, this is*
> *the best season of your life.*

"This might sound grandiose to you, Al, but I
think Nancy and I would have had a hard time trading in the last year of her life for something else, even
if we knew, in the bargain, that Nancy would live
longer—or live forever." I'm glad the choice was not
ours to make, I said.

"I know exactly what you mean," said Al. "It's
hard to talk about this to someone who hasn't been

through it. They assume that being around dying is
depressing.

"I always assumed that the reason Diane and I
had such an intimately rich time together was precisely because we *knew* that she would die. For two
years, we lived knowing this would be our last trip
to Sausalito, our last Thanksgiving together with the
whole family, the last hike to Gooseberry Falls during the height of autumn colors on the North Shore.
We knew that there was no time to go to a boring
cocktail party with business associates or watch
junk TV."

It was almost two o'clock. The Crystal Room was
largely empty, but the staff was much too polite to
make us feel hurried. I ordered a pot of tea.

"Maybe you don't need to *know* death looms
around the bend," I conjectured. "Perhaps just being
around the possibility of death heightens the intensity of living."

"It's an interesting theory," replied Al. "But if
you're right, doctors and nurses would be enlight-
ened beings living in some kind of elevated state."

"OK, then. How *do* you explain it?" I asked.

Al shook his head. He carved a circular indenta-
tion in the tablecloth with his spoon.

"It's a mystery. After Diane's diagnosis, *everything*
was suddenly a mystery."

Al lifted the spoon to his lips. "I suppose that

because the territory was mysterious, we were forced to pay attention. I know that when I pay really close attention to something, space opens up to make even the most mundane things appear magical. Our last two years together were certainly that—magical.

"And then there's the process of caring for another by attending to her most minuscule needs," Al continued. Al said he'd dressed Diane. He'd bathed her. Paradoxically, as his focus shifted away from himself, he felt enlivened, not depleted, he said.

"Diane's condition didn't separate us," Al explained. "It was not as if she were the 'sick' one and I the 'well' one. It was not as if she were the 'patient' and I the 'caregiver.' In retrospect, I recognize that everything I did for Diane, I was doing to take care of myself. I was being my own caregiver by being attentive to her with such immediacy."

Al sighed and gazed out the window. He said he tried to use the same approach in his relationship with his son, whom he hadn't talked to for over a year. But his attempt was a failure.

"If our minds think we're experts, we bring our old baggage to the new situation. Our cups become filled with an accumulation of our prior experiences, reactions, judgments, expectations, and assumptions. Eventually there's no room left for newness, even when something *is* new."

"So, you're saying this is a 'once in a lifetime' experience," I said.

"I don't know. I do know that, for me, being with Diane after she got a terminal diagnosis profoundly changed my life . . ."

Al gave no indication that he was going to continue his thought. We both sat in silence for a while. I was surprised that silence felt comfortable in the setting of a luncheon club for the Minneapolis business elite.

"So let me repeat what I heard you to be saying," I said after the second time our server asked if there was anything else she could get us. "Being a caregiver was new to both of us. We both jumped into it with passion, taking time off from our regular jobs and routines to attend to caring for our wives. Our relationships deepened. We experienced magic. We lived in a mystery. You think it was the newness of the experience that gave it aliveness. And you can't bring that same air of mystery to the relationship with your son."

Al nodded. "Now that you push me on this, I'm seeing that, with my son, I was trying to force the situation. I think that if I'd stepped back and just been in awe of the unfolding of the complexity of a relationship between an adult son and his father, it might have been different. I came to my relationship with him with preconceived ideas. Perhaps I need to get the ideas out of my head and live in its mystery."

With death, mystery is not an issue, is it, Nancy? What can be more mysterious than death? We don't know even the most basic things about it. By focusing on the medical event that occurs at death, we really miss the mark, don't we. We forget that what is happening hasn't been fully explained by any scientist, philosopher, or theologian. Death brings into focus the most basic questions: who are we? what is it to be? how do we know what we know?—questions for which we have no answers. Perhaps it's precisely when we live these questions day to day that we experience vitality.

I first lived these questions when I was struggling with my meningitis. I told Al how the treatments consisted of injecting amphotericin B—a drug that has been likened to battery acid—into the back of my head where the spinal cord ends. How it irritates everything around—including the nerve endings that come together at the base of the skull where I received the injections. That sometimes I'd suffer loss of vision or loss of hearing. That once I had paraplegia for almost two days. That nausea and vomiting were routine. And that the reactions were due, in part, to elevated pulse, blood pressure, and body temperature from a chemical reaction to amphotericin B.

"With those kinds of reactions," I said, "it's customary to administer narcotics to get a patient through the treatments. But with treatments every other day, I felt that the residual effect of the narcotics put me in a perpetual 'Gumby'-like state. I began to search for alternatives. Quite by chance, I happened upon what, I subsequently learned, was a kind of primitive biofeedback. I paid very close attention to my pulse, my blood pressure, and my body temperature. I got to the point that I actually experienced the flow of blood inside an artery and felt the pressure exerted on its walls. I experienced body temperature not just on the surface of my skin but in my muscles and organs. Inexplicably, my pulse, blood pressure, and body temperature would self-correct. There were times that my pulse and blood pressure were at healthier levels after a treatment than before. My reactions to the treatments diminished. Eventually, I was able to eliminate the use of the narcotics almost completely.

"My mind immediately raced to solutions. I thought I had figured things out: if I intentionally lower my pulse and my blood pressure, the painful reactions to the treatments will disappear. All I've got to do is to focus on forcing my blood pressure and pulse lower.

"The moment I started doing that, things fell

apart. I could no more *force* my pulse or my blood pressure than I could *force* my mind to stop thinking. My improved reactions came to an abrupt halt.

"Seeing that having 'answers' wasn't working, I went back to just paying intimate attention to my pulse and blood pressure without trying to force a result. I just experienced the sensation of blood in a vein or an artery. I allowed myself to be present to the sensation of pressure on their walls. I just paid attention.

"The moment I did that, my pulse and blood pressure would mysteriously self-correct. The pain would diminish."

Al did not nod. He did not smile. He just sat. Then, he leaned over the table, touched my hand, and said just one word: "Control.

"It's the illusion of control," he continued after sitting back. "You were not in control. I was not in control. The doctors were not in control. There was some inner 'presence' that was all knowing. The 'presence' was within us but was not us. It's a total mystery to me."

It is for me, too, Nancy.

Is it Oz?

with all my love,

*Dear
Nancy,*

Last week, my grief group went on a weekend retreat. The session started much like our regular weekly meetings—a speaker addressed an aspect of grief and then invited us to share from our own experience. But this time, after the "check-in," the facilitator, Stuart, introduced an exercise.

A caregiver is faced with principally one thing only, said Stuart. The loss of the life of a loved one. But the dying person is facing multiple losses: possessions, activities, interpersonal roles. The exercise is designed to simulate the losses experienced by the dying person, he informed us.

Stuart handed each of us a pencil and sixteen index cards—four blue, four green, four pink, and four white. On the blue cards, he asked us to name the four objects most precious to us.

For me, the first was the woods at our wilderness retreat. Then the oil portrait of you painted by your brother that we displayed at your memorial service. It now hangs above the desk in my study where I write these letters. The other objects were more difficult to prioritize—picture albums, the Rainis painting my parents had brought with them from Latvia.

The green cards were for the four activities that I love most: negotiating deals, writing, lumberjacking, reading. The pink cards were for my four most important roles: father, advisor, seeker, and caregiver. The white cards for the four living people most dear to me: Julia, Mac, my mother, and my sister Dana. Stuart told us to arrange the sixteen cards in front of us. They constituted the world that was most precious to us.

"Death will take one card from each category," announced Stuart. "Select one thing, one activity, one role, and one person. I am going to play the role of Death and come around to collect the cards you choose. What you hand over to me, you hand to Death. Death does not take you. You continue to live, but you will have to live without that activity, role, thing, and person."

My skin became prickly. I knew this was "just" an exercise. Yet it seemed so real. These were *my* loved ones, *my* activities, *my* roles, and *my* things—not just some abstract notion.

I quickly realized that it wasn't the four cards Stuart demanded I relinquish that were causing me pain. It was the anticipation of the next four. How could I make a choice between my remaining loved

ones—Julia, Mac, and Dana? Difficult as it was to
hand over my mother to Stuart's outstretched hand,
she was ninety-two and had lived a full life. But
how could I possibly choose among the remaining
three? I would have to choose my sister, I reasoned.
But what then? A choice between our son, Mac,
and our daughter, Julia. That was impossible! How
could Stuart ask me to make that choice, even in an
exercise? Why hadn't I been clever enough to put
Julia and Mac on one card labeled "children," rather
than list them individually by name? My forehead
became hot.

But as so often seems to happen, the dreaded
never materialized. Instead, Stuart announced that
Death would randomly select cards in the next round
of losses. Death might take some. Death might take
all. Death might take from some categories and not
from others. "Think about it," Stuart directed. "You
might be left with all your loved ones, but lose every
one of your roles and activities. What would that
be like for you—to have the loved ones in your life
without any of your familiar roles?"

"Such loss often happens to people who are in
the process of dying," he continued. "They still have
their loved ones, but they've lost all of the important
roles they played in their lives and the lives of their
loved ones. Some people are bedridden and lose all
of the activities that defined them. Others move to

a nursing home or a hospice and lose their dearest possessions."

"What a relief," I sighed. I recognized that the pain I'd been experiencing had little to do with the loss of the four cards that I'd just handed over to Death—little to do with real losses. My suffering had been created by the anticipation of pain to come. I took a deep breath and relaxed. I'd been seduced into worrying about the future.

Nancy, I started to recall the many moments when you and I were tricked into dreading future possibilities rather than staying present to immediate actualities. I remember the scores of cisternal punctures I endured for the treatment of my meningitis. Only after dozens of injections did I realize that the pain of the needle ripping through the soft skin at the back of my neck was minimal compared to the anxiety of anticipating the pain. I worried that loss of my vision, loss of hearing, and paraplegia would be permanent, not temporary as we'd been assured by the neurosurgeon.

Eventually I learned that if I stayed present to the pain of the needle exactly where it was—not where it might be—the treatment was less traumatic. "Stay present to the pain," you'd coach me. "Don't resist it. Breathe. Breathe in the pain you are experiencing right at this moment. Where do you feel the needle just now? Describe for me exactly what it feels like."

Your instructions guided me back to the simple reality of a needle tearing through soft tissue. The pain didn't disappear. But the suffering did.

Yet, when it came to your cancer, all too often I would forget to stay in the present. "What if you have an allergic reaction to Taxol or sisplatinum?" My mind raced. "What if the physician punctures your lung while removing fluid from the pleural space?" My mind raced faster. "What if the nasal respirator fails and you need the ventilator again? The pain and discomfort of the tube in your trachea had been so unbearable. How could you endure being intubated again?"

We'd clutch each other, holding our breaths as we tumbled into the dark unknown of possible outcomes, flailing like Alice falling into Wonderland. I groped for guideposts. More data. More opinions. More thinking about what might possibly come, forgetting to be present to where we were. Then I'd remember the experience of my meningitis, and I'd begin to do for you what you had done for me.

"Breathe, Nancy," I'd counsel. "Ease into the pain that you feel right at this moment. Where exactly do you feel it? Can you describe it? Does it have a color? Blue? Red? Does it have a texture? Sharp? Diffuse? Does it have a shape?

"Stay present to the pain that's right here. You

know you can handle the pain that is real. Don't resist the pain, Nancy. Let it in."

You'd open yourself to the pain. It would dissolve enough for you to take my hand. "The mind plays such tricks, doesn't it," you once observed after a surgery. "Our minds are so busy. Forever racing to future possibilities. Even with all of the work you and I have done on staying in the present, my mind still keeps wanting to leap elsewhere. Though I know that I'd much rather experience the feel of your hand holding mine, my mind still races off into the myriad 'what ifs.'"

"What if we were to let go of all of the 'what ifs'?" I recall asking you. "What then?"

"All those 'what ifs'—the anticipation of what might be but isn't—are what make up the ego," you replied. "If we were to let go of the 'what ifs,' the ego would have nothing left to do. Our egos would die."

I called Stuart. What about the ego? I asked. No one in our group mentioned the ego as precious. What about the loss of that?

"Would that be a loss?"

His question was rhetorical.

with all my love,

Dear
Nancy,

  A couple of months ago, my friend George invited me to a two-and-a-half-day meditation retreat—a *sesshin*—with his Zen teacher. A weekend out of town would give me a chance to spend time with George. And I was eager to develop a formal meditation practice. I accepted George's invitation.

  George said that this *sesshin* was intended for beginners. Even so, except for an hour-long *dharma* lecture, the entire day—from six-thirty in the morning until nine at night—was spent in silence. We sat on small hard cushions for thirty minutes. Then a bell would chime, and we'd walk for ten minutes in silence around the perimeter of the meditation hall, methodically placing one foot in front of the other. Then back to sitting. Even meals were served *oryoki* style—in silence at our meditation cushions with our legs crossed. "Stay present," were the instructions. "Don't let your mind wander. Bring it back to your breath. Bring it back to your body."

  It took less than a couple of hours for my knees

to ache and for my back to burn with pain. I began to fidget. I was desperate to move around, to get out doors. Anything—and everything—began to distract me. A bus, blocks away, barely audible. A mosquito in the far corner of the hall. Another participant quietly rearranging herself on her cushion by a fraction of an inch. I was unable to keep my thoughts from racing to responsibilities at work, at home, anywhere but my breath. My knees screamed with pain. I felt razorblades pushing against my scapula. If I didn't move to relieve the pressure, I felt they'd sever my spinal cord.

Participants were given the opportunity to meet with the head teacher, the *roshi*. These personal interviews, *dokusan*, were intended to give students an opportunity to discuss their practice one on one. When the *roshi*'s assistant tapped my shoulder, gesturing for an indication of whether I wished *dokusan*, I quickly rose and followed the assistant to the *roshi*'s private chamber.

"I'm miserable," I said to the *roshi*.

He nodded.

"My back hurts. My knees ache. This seems so silly to me—contrived pain."

The *roshi* sat in silence. He was not going to make it easy for me.

"I know about staying present," I said. "I'm not

a guy who avoids facing suffering. But painful knees and an aching back seem so trivial. I've known *real* suffering."

The *roshi* did not ask me how I happened to know "real" suffering. He sat, his legs crossed, his eyes penetrating my essence. I offered an explanation anyway.

I told him about your cancer, and how I stayed present through every surgery, every chemotherapy, every painful recovery. I told him about my coccidioidal meningitis, and how I stayed present to every intrathecal injection and its neurological side effects of paraplegia, loss of vision, loss of hearing, and vomiting. Working on staying present to aching knees, I said, seemed to me like working out with five-pound weights. I'd already been lifting three hundred.

The *roshi* finally spoke. He spoke eloquently about life, about death, about kindness, about staying present—to pain and to pleasure—and about how subtle are the games that the mind plays. He turned my thinking upside down.

Staying present to a dying wife is no three-hundred-pound weight, was the implication of what he said. I had no real choice. I was attentive and patient because I *had* to be. Would I do the same with the inattentive store clerk? With the persistent

telemarketer? I could stay present to the pain of amphotericin B injections. I had to. But did I have the
discipline to gently hold the pain in my crossed legs?

I recall your saying that if you died, you'd have
few regrets. Julia was, to use your words, "launched."
Mac's self-confidence would "see him through."

If you died, what you would regret, you told
me, is not being present for Julia's and Mac's life
passages—Julia's graduation from college, Mac's moving into an apartment of his own, Julia's wedding,
your first grandchild.

You knew, didn't you, that surgery and chemo
were five-pound weights compared to the three-
hundred-pound weight of missing celebrations. I
wish I had known, Nancy, how to help you lift that
weight.

with all my love,

PERCEPTION

from *Gifts of Spirit;* spiritual growth
group meditation, April 18, 1996

I don't know if you ever saw the incredibly fun movie
with Marlon Brando and Johnny Depp, a very gifted
new actor, and Faye Dunaway, called *Don Juan de
Marcos.* Johnny Depp is a young man who thinks he is
Don Juan, and he romances women. Marlon Brando is
a psychiatrist who takes him seriously.

Don Juan says, "It is all a matter of perception.
Some may say that one woman has a nose that is too
large, or another feature that is too short, but I do not
look at those things at all. I see the radiant jewel that
lives within each woman; the gorgeous, unique beauty
at her core. And she responds to my vision by expressing that great beauty."

That is the secret. If you really can perceive the
beauty, that is what comes out. This allows us to live a
life filled with love. It is very subtle and slow, but it is
just true, that our perception creates what we get in our
lives. It is a basic law: "As within, so without." If you
have people in your lives that are critical and judgmental and impatient, it reflects that there is something in
you that is like that.

Just as we are what we eat—if we eat good calories of healthful food, we have good blood chemistry. If we eat junk food, it eventually catches up with us, and we don't have good inner health. And that is also true of mental food. What we eat mentally, what we take into our minds and we digest, becomes our life. It is so crucial to really be aware of what you are eating in terms of your thoughts, and go on a mental health food love diet today. The more you feast on love, the more love there will to be to feast on.

This is something that is very real and very serious. . . . So we need to be serious about what we want in life and say, "We can do this."

But at the same time, we have to realize that this is very difficult. Unfortunately, the minute you get to one level, you are going to be challenged to another level. So it is really wonderful to keep humility in mind. In fact, all the great spiritual warriors tell us that humility and vulnerability are essential attributes. Be kind to yourself when you slip into your old habits of being mad and critical; don't be too hard on yourself.

Dear
Nancy,

Last week my mother tripped going up the stairs to her bedroom and hurt her arm. Although no bones were broken and she doesn't wear a sling any more, she can elevate her right hand only with the help of the left. Nancy, you know my mother would never complain. But I suspect she's in pain. She needs help getting dressed—and with anything else that requires both hands. Yesterday, I stood at the bathroom sink with her after dinner and helped her wash her hands.

The last time I washed my mother's hands was the day after your memorial service. My mother, your brother and sisters, their families, my sisters, your godson Chad, and your closest friends, Bonnie and Therese, all drove up in caravan to our Wisconsin retreat. For me, the two-and-a-half-hour drive along familiar country roads felt soothing after the intensity of the memorial service.

Although no agenda had been formally discussed, we all understood what we would do: we'd walk in silence to Spring Lake Creek, tracing the steps that you'd walked so many times along this narrow trail. We'd listen to the quiet of the northern Wisconsin woods that you so loved. We'd scatter the ashes of your remains in Spring Lake Creek. One by one, we'd place flowers in the creek. And then, after the walk of almost five miles round-trip, I'd wash the hands of all those present.

My friend Kevin suggested the hand-washing ritual. It's an old Persian custom for the householder to wash the hands of each grieving guest before he returns to his everyday chores, he said. "Your guests will have carried much more than the ashes of Nancy's remains. They'll need closure and release. They'll be nurtured by having their burdens washed away."

My sister Dana found a flowered ceramic bowl in my mother's basement. Its inside was sculptured, like a seashell. The outside was decorated in an intricate lace pattern. Though delicate in appearance, the bowl was heavy—and nearly thick enough to be a sink. After Dana discovered the bowl and brought it over to show me, I placed my hands in it and visualized how another pair of hands would fit together with mine.

My mother supplied a large cut-glass pitcher for the cold water. For warm water we used the bright

yellow jug Julia made in clay camp when she was
twelve. Dana and I placed the bowls and pitchers
on a wooden table outdoors in the clearing below
the deck and laid out separate towels for each of the
thirty guests.

Washing thirty pairs of hands, one at a time, took
nearly two hours. I'd have been happy to have it take
all day! Holding a hand in silence and massaging its
palms was a contact with our friends and relatives
I'd never experienced before. In the soapy lukewarm
water, each hand had a unique sensuality, a distinct
texture. Long and bony fingers for some. Pudgy
knuckles for others. Nancy, there is so much more
to the thumb than the part that extends beyond the
palm. Its muscles can be felt all the way to the wrist.
Your brother's hands. My mother's hands. Your niece
Amy's hands. Each so remarkably different. Open
hands. Giving hands. Accepting hands. At the same
time, each so remarkably the same.

I noticed that for each person, the rhythm of
the hand washing was distinct. Some hands were no-
ticeably tense at the start of this unfamiliar Middle
Eastern ritual. But after just a few seconds in the
warm, nurturing water, the hands invariably relaxed.
I usually found myself looking in the eyes of the
person whose hands I was washing, not at the hands
being washed. It almost seemed like what was being

washed was visible there, behind the eyes, not in the soapy water below. Washing became almost ancillary. An inner cleansing was occurring.

After I'd washed all thirty pairs of hands, my mother washed my hands. Now it was she who looked behind my eyes. She gave me a knowing look, then smiled. I thanked her. Neither of us had to say anything about having experienced your presence and our interconnectedness.

Now, six months later, as I washed my mother's hands once again, I noticed her hands had changed. They were more fragile. "Just let them soak for a minute," I said. "The warm water will relieve the pain."

I began to remove my hands, but before I could withdraw them, she gently closed her good hand around mine, holding them in the basin, and looked into my eyes. "It's not the warmth of the water, son, that soothes the pain."

with all my love,

EFFERVESCENCE

*Dear
Nancy,*

My life has become like carbonated water gone flat. Still drinkable. But missing its character.

From the moment we were told your shortness of breath was not a natural result of your having just entered the fifth decade of your life, effervescence permeated everything. In that one moment, life stopped being table water. Everything tingled. I feel ashamed to admit that I miss effervescence almost as much as I miss you.

I had lunch again the other day with our friend John, who spent two tours of duty in Vietnam. He said he could completely identify with my sense of flatness. Though he himself never took a bullet in Vietnam, death stared him in the face moment to moment. His best buddies were killed. When he was there, he was scared and couldn't wait for it to be over. Yet, when he returned, he missed the atmosphere charged with adrenaline.

"That was almost thirty years ago," said John. "But I remember it like it was yesterday. I've never been as alive as when I was in the constant presence of death. But it wasn't the 'real' world."

I never suspected that your death was staring us in the face. But after your diagnosis, the fragility of life was omnipresent. In hospital emergency rooms. Surgical recovery waiting rooms. Chemotherapy wards. Adrenaline added carbonation to every swallow that I took. I miss the tingle of immediacy.

You died in June. Yet the effervescence was still there in July, August, and September. It was there in October and into November. Then something started to happen. The intensity changed. I started just going through the days. I had not become depressed, I don't believe. But I had reentered the "real" world. I started to see brick walls, not what's on the other side of them. I rejoined a community in which material monism is the accepted worldview.

Nancy, is that all there is to it? Changing one's worldview? Knowing that there is more than the brick wall? Nancy, help me to reconnect to a worldview that allows me to feel effervescence in every moment that is lived.

with all my love,

Dear
    Nancy,

While Mac, Julia, and I were skiing in Colorado last week, my office was burglarized. Expensive laptop computers and calculators were left untouched. But the thieves rifled through desk drawers and took all the cash and blank checks they could find. When I returned, I discovered that my checkbook and register were missing.

I was angry. With the register missing, I'll have to re-create a whole year of financial records. And with tax season coming up, I can't even put off the inevitable hassle of rebuilding the records until later! I'd gladly have given the burglars cash if they'd agree to return the register. But first, I had to deal with the missing checks.

I called our banker, Doug, to close the account. "No problem," he said. "You'll have checks for your new account within a week. Will you want everything the same on the new checks as on your old ones?"

I paused. Though it's been almost a year since you died, the checks I use still read, "Andris A. or

Nancy J. Baltins." I suddenly realized that Doug's question had implications greater than color, style, and font.

The last time I recall addressing the issue of how we designate our funds was almost thirty years ago. "What about checking accounts?" I recall you asking on our honeymoon. "Now that we're married, we can't continue to keep separate accounts."

"How will we keep things straight?" I responded. If we both write checks on the same account, checks will be out of sequence, I reasoned. It will become impossible to keep track. We'll end up having arguments.

"If we're a single unit legally and a single unit spiritually, how can we be separate units financially?" you said. "This isn't just a matter of convenience. It's a symbol of how we relate to each other and to the community."

Of course your logic carried the day. We pooled our scant resources and opened a new account. But it lasted as "our" account for only a year or so. I'd been right. Checks were out of sequence. The register was a mess.

We opened a second account that was just yours. You were still a signatory on our joint account, but you'd write only an occasional check on the joint account to replenish your own. Even that was maddening. You'd forget to tell me about the checks you'd written on our joint account, and I'd be unable to balance the account. I'd try to persuade you that if you didn't keep track of the checks you wrote, the account might be overdrawn and checks would bounce.

"Doug at the bank knows us," you'd respond. "He'd never bounce my checks. If I'm overdrawn, he'll call me first."

After running out of logical arguments, I'd say, "You're an accountant's daughter. What would your father say?"

"There's only so much time in life," you'd respond. "I have to choose what is meaningful to me. I choose to have confidence in the people we deal with. My bank is one of them. Being accurate to the penny is just not a priority for me. Andy, if you feel the need to balance your checkbook to feel comfortable, you should do it for your own satisfaction. But it's not for me."

Even though I never found a bank error in my own statements, I would regale you with stories of bank errors from others. I would even stoop to appealing to your feminism and argue that if women are to be independent, they need to take responsibility for financial matters. Nothing worked. The fact that our housekeeper did in fact write checks on your account for over a year, a little bit at a time, made no difference. "She must have really needed the money badly to steal from me in that way. I can't caretake her," you replied.

I let go of haranguing only because I became exhausted, not because I could understand your approach. I balanced my checkbook before the sun set on the day a statement came in the mail. What delight to make my account balance come out to the penny! I could devote hours to justifying a discrepancy of just a couple of dollars. It never occurred to me that accepting the bank's balance, especially since it was already within pennies of my own, was an acceptable alternative. It was like brushing your teeth in the morning. It was not something to contemplate or negotiate. It was a given.

Isn't it paradoxical that since you died, I haven't balanced the checkbook once? Not only haven't I balanced the checkbook, I have yet to open the statements. A whole year's worth of them piled up! Unimaginable to me a year ago.

Nancy, I now see that you were right—we give our time and attention to the things that we value. Having my register balance match the bank's to the penny is no longer a priority. I now recognize that there will come a day when someone else is writing checks on my account, as I am on what was ours.

Suddenly, Doug's question about the style, color, and lettering for a new account took on more significant implications. This was not just a simple decision about whether or not to remove your name from the blank checks that were to be printed. The closing of the account was the closing of a life together.

"What would happen if I don't close the account?" I asked the banker. "Can I just keep the same account until we find out if someone is really trying to pass off the checks as mine?"

"Closing the account won't stop someone from writing checks on the account. If a merchant accepts a check without proper identification, it's the merchant's risk, not yours or the bank's," said Doug. "But the account has been compromised. It would be our advice that you close it, but it's your decision."

I decided not to close the account. Keeping our old account alive would force me to balance it, though I might perhaps reconsider the need to have it accurate to the penny. Keeping our old account alive would also remind me that it continued to represent our joint funds, not something just mine. But I did decide that it was time to change the name. Keeping your name on the checks, I reasoned, would be like keeping the gold heart-in-the-hand pendant that was cremated with your body: holding on to an artifice.

with all my love,

Dear
Nancy,

Our decision to scatter your cremated remains in Spring Lake Creek seemed self-evident at
the time. Why, I wonder, do I feel the need to justify
that decision now? In the wake of your death, I didn't
consider alternatives or deliberate. I allowed myself
to be pulled along by a tether of unfolding moments.
I heard answers to questions I'd not asked. And one
of those answers was Spring Lake Creek—the creek
that runs through the northern part of our wilderness retreat in Wisconsin. The creek you'd hike to
and sit at the side of, regardless of weather, regardless of time constraints. We were meant to scatter
your ashes there.

It was a hot July afternoon. The thermometer
had edged over 90° well before noon. I wouldn't
be surprised if the humidity was over 90 percent as
well. Not even a wisp of a breeze. This, the land of
marshes, bogs, wetlands, and lakes, had become a
tropical rain forest.

Your brother Jim, his wife, and my mother

decided that the two-mile walk through the narrow tree-covered trails would be too taxing. At our
home, by the lake, it only *felt* like a tropical rain
forest. In the thick, uncut woods, it would also *look*
like one. They stayed home. The rest of us walked.
Slowly. Even so, we had to stop frequently to rest and
take turns carrying the heavy Grecian urn you and I
had bought from a street vendor in the ancient section of Corinth. He'd somehow convinced us that
its weight was not a problem. It was evidence of its
authenticity, he said.

The urn had been designed centuries ago to carry
water. For ten years it had been an objet d'art in our
living room. Last July it became the receptacle for
your cremated remains. Now, it sits on the credenza
in my study. I marvel at its intricate geometric design
as I write this letter to you and wonder if it will have
yet more incarnations. It's no longer a water jug. It's
no longer an objet d'art. It's no longer a vessel for
your cremated body. What is it? Is it defined by what
it was intended for? By what it was used for? By the
memories with which it's imbued?

I suppose that burying your ashes at Lakewood
Cemetery would have been the "natural" thing to
do. Perhaps then, Rob and Clarise from the Drop-In
Center wouldn't have had a reason to confront me
with questions. "Why is there no *place* for Nancy?"
asked Clarise. "Where is she considered to be

buried?" Rob demanded. Where could they pay
respects to you, they wanted to know. Clarise even
questioned if God approved of what he referred to as
a "dispersing" of you—and whether what we'd done
might be "unsanitary." She looked at me as if I, not
she, might be the one with autism.

Rob and Clarise were not mollified by my references to dust returning to dust. Rob straightened
his glasses—Nancy, he still wears the black ones that
are taped with white surgical tape on one bow—and
with his arms crossed and legs stiff in a Marine ser-
geant stance, pronounced in his booming deep voice
that it's *meant* that there be a marker to show where
dead people rest. "And it's just plain *no good* if it's
not in a clearly identified place."

I reasoned to Rob and Clarise that they could
pay respects to you anywhere—and everywhere.
That you were present deep within their hearts. I
also allowed that there were rumors that a stained-
glass window might be dedicated in your memory
at Plymouth Church. Unsatisfied by my reply, Rob
turned on his heel and strode to the coffee urn,
maintaining his military posture. Clarise and Rob
wanted something truly solid. A granite tombstone
over your physical remains, not some diaphanous
symbol that might be dedicated to you but wasn't *you*.

I suppose it's true that Rob and Clarise can pay
respects to you anywhere. It's equally true that you're

in their hearts—and in the hearts of every other
member of the Drop-In Center, which you served,
nurtured, and preserved for nearly twenty years. It's
true that a stained-glass window will be dedicated in
your memory at Plymouth Church. Yet those are not
reasons that justify Spring Lake Creek. The truth is,
Spring Lake Creek called. I responded.

Spring Lake Creek has an inauspicious start—
through a culvert that runs under County Road E.
Spring Lake's massive body of water pushes against
the tiny culvert with the weight of hundreds of millions of Grecian urns. Not even fallen tree trunks
and branches are able to block the flow of the creek
west through our land and over to the Namekagon
River.

The Namekagon runs south into the St. Croix
River, which, in turn, empties into the Mississippi.
The Mississippi River, of course, flows into the Gulf
of Mexico and the Atlantic Ocean. Air evaporates
from the Atlantic and forms clouds that release their
moisture everywhere. I suppose some of that moisture even falls on Spring Lake and then runs again
down our creek, making a complete cycle.

The walk to Spring Lake Creek would take us
along the sleigh trail, cleared by lumberjacks in the
1890s, through the fir glade, the stand of towering
virgin pine, along the tamarack in the low land to a
small log bridge hewn by Hank from a massive white

pine that fell across the creek years ago. I stood alone on the log, the urn in one hand balanced with the other against a frail birch railing. Bright blue water rushed below. Orange, brown, and gray pebbles were clearly visible through the foot or two of water.

Propped cautiously against the railing, I shifted my weight and began to pour ashes from the urn. They seemed to hang for a moment in the air and then drifted into the creek. Finer particles were immediately carried down the creek. Larger ones settled below the log bridge, creating an oval of light gray juxtaposed to the reddish brown pebbles and the mossy rock.

Your sister Margie placed the rose she'd carried into the creek. It soon caught on a rock. Reaching down from the log bridge, I was able to free it. But it soon caught again. Mac threw his rose into the rushing current beyond the rock on which Margie's had caught. His rose drifted nearly to the bend before catching against a mossy boulder. Therese started peeling the petals off her rose and placing them one by one into the current. Janey, Chad, and Evan followed her lead. Soon the creek was dotted with rose petals. We joined hands and sang "Shall We Gather at the River?"

When we had finished, Julia unexpectedly lay down in the creek. She loosely stretched her arms. The spring water ran over her. I watched her blond hair and long, light cotton dress flow with the current. Her dress clung to her body. She appeared ghostlike in the clear waters of the creek. I was startled, yet mesmerized. What was she doing?

For a moment, I feared she was joining her mother. Should I be rescuing her? I stood, motionless, crouched on the log bridge, holding the empty urn, staring into the rushing water filled with your ashes, with rose petals, and, now, with Julia. The bright blues and greens of her long dress seemed to dissolve into the greens of the algae and moss. Like the finer particles of your cremated remains, her finer particles seemed to fuse with the water of the creek, ready to wash into the Namekagon and out to the Atlantic. Like your heavier particles, a part of her remained in the creek bed. Our beloved pristine creek was suddenly filled with elements that were not Spring Lake Creek. I wondered if your ashes, the rose petals, and my anxiety about Julia had become part of the creek and in some way now made up the creek.

On reflection, I realize that Spring Lake Creek is made up *solely* of elements that are *not* Spring Lake Creek. It is made up of rocks and pebbles from the ice age, of sand eroded from the banks of our land. It is made up of water from Spring Lake and fallen trees, of moss growing on rocks. And since July 1996, Spring Lake Creek is also made up of perspiration from Julia's body and the ashes of your body. Is it also made up of my memories of the rituals observed there a week after your death?

Last week, I was walking with Mac along the Atlantic coast at Key West. A pebble or perhaps the fragment of a conch shimmered in the afternoon sun. I reached down to pick it up. But as I bent over, a wave broke, and what had shimmered a moment before was suddenly covered in water and foam. The wave receded, leaving a section of brownish green algae and half of a well-weathered tiller washed up against my foot.

At first I wanted to label the tiller and the algae as flotsam, debris separate from the ocean. Then I saw Mac methodically pouring the rest of his soda into the receding wave and was reminded that the Atlantic Ocean, like Spring Lake Creek, is made up solely of elements that are something else—it's made up of Mac's soda, water from the Mississippi, wrecks of the *Titanic* and *Andrea Doria,* ashes of your remains, Julia's perspiration, fragments of conch shells and pebbles, the origins of which are too diverse to imagine. Is there anything that's made up of just *itself,* not of an infinitude of *other* things?

Mac and I left the beach. The sand was ashen hot. The salty residue of the ocean water on my ankles

felt like concentrated perspiration from Julia's body.
I turned to Mac. Do you ever wonder what *we're*
made up of? I asked.

"Memories," he replied without hesitation.

with all my love,

Dear
Nancy,

Lately, I've been aware that deaths are occurring everywhere around me. Not just *people* dying. I notice that *everything* is impermanent and is in the process of dying. My friends don't seem to see things the same way. Or at least they're not willing to talk about it.

In any event, I feel alone. It's as if I have some paranormal lens implant that causes me to see reality differently than do any of my friends. Even my old friend Dan didn't identify with my sense of loss as we played our final tennis match this afternoon at the Northstar tennis club, which, tomorrow, will close for good. My conversation with Dan is still on my mind.

"You're sure quiet this afternoon," Dan said to me. "You depressed?"

"No. I'm fine," I responded. "Just thinking."

"About what?"

"I've been thinking about how we've been playing tennis at four o'clock on Wednesdays on Court No. 3 for twenty years. Same court. Same time.

Every week for twenty years. We know each other's game so well, we don't really play tennis anymore. Instead, it's as if we're engaged in a dance—a dance in which the steps and moves have been choreographed ahead of time. We're tango dancers, Dan, not tennis players."

Dan has had to endure listening to me philosophize before. He knew there was no point in trying to divert me. He dressed in silence.

"And now, after all these years, they're going to put an office building here," I continued. "Some fancy marble security desk will be located here where our lockers are today. Doors to an elevator bank will replace the door to the sauna. There will be no court. There will be no net. We must have hit literally hundreds of thousands, maybe millions, of balls across the net on Court No. 3 over these twenty years. And now it'll be gone."

"So?" Dan rolled his eyes but said nothing.

"I'm not just heavy-hearted about the loss of our court." I unlaced my street shoes. "We all knew that this club couldn't stay here forever. It sits on real estate that's much too valuable for a tennis club. I suppose we should be surprised that it's lived this long, not that it's finally dying." What I didn't say is that I'm beginning to understand that *everything* is in a constant state of change—that everything dies and something new is born in its place.

The locker room clock read 3:55. The clock has been ten minutes fast for as long as either of us can remember. We still had a good quarter of an hour before our court time.

"The young guys who played tennis on Court 3 at four o'clock twenty years ago, those guys died long ago. Right? The men who'll play there today are completely different people. Twenty years ago you were married. Your marriage died. Fifteen years ago, you were running for office for the first time. Your political career died. Ten years ago, you hadn't even considered going back to school and becoming a psychologist. We had full heads of hair. Each of us weighed twenty pounds less. It might as well have been guys with different names that were registered for this court at four o'clock twenty years ago, or ten years ago, or even last week. You know, Dan, who we are dies moment to moment."

Dan closed the door to his locker. "It's not that long since Nancy died," he said. "A significant loss triggers depression. It's part of the territory. It's a normal reaction to the loss of a loved one. How you *handle* depression is what matters."

Dan glanced up at the clock. "Why don't we head out to the court and hit a couple of balls? You'll feel a lot better once you get a workout. Get some exercise. You'll get over it."

We proceeded from the men's locker room to

Court No. 3. Past Glenda at the registration desk, who, as always, was talking on the phone. Waving to the seniors doubles group from Court No. 2, who had, as always, finished early and were already chatting. Down the half flight of stairs. We'd taken each of these steps countless times before and out on to the green asphalt surface of Court No. 3. The net was raised at the doubles lines by worn wooden slats. Everything was the same as it had been last week, the week before, the year before.

Yet one thing was not the same this Wednesday from four o'clock to five thirty: tennis was not the same. I listened to the momentary crisp thud as the strings of my racket met the ball. I allowed each volley to die, and I moved on, giving the present volley undivided attention. Then I listened to the absence of a thud being replaced by the sound of Dan's shoes reversing direction on the court as he lunged to retrieve a shot. I delighted in the contrast between the neon yellow of the ball and the jet black lettering of the ball manufacturer's name. I marveled at how the lettering blurred when the ball was spinning toward me and how rigidly it froze at the moment it was about to leave the strings.

"That was some pretty terrific tennis you played today," Dan raved at the end of the match. "I can't remember when we played a better set. That point in the tiebreak, when I was up 5-3, was incredible. You retrieved that overhead shot which should've been a put away, and you came back with that forehand cross-court to win. I can't say I liked losing, but the match was terrific! How's your depression now? You still brooding about death? I bet that workout put you back to rights."

We undressed and headed for the sauna. As always, we picked up a couple of Styrofoam cups, filled them with water, and poured the water on the hot sauna rocks. As always, steam shot up from the sauna furnace, momentarily obfuscating the sign that reads, DO NOT POUR WATER—RISK OF ELECTRICAL SHOCK. We laid out towels on the hot wooden bench. I was ready to "de-brief."

"I do feel good," I said. "That was lots of fun. And you're right. I don't feel depressed."

I poured another cup of water on the rocks. "But I wonder which is the chicken and which is the egg. Maybe it was the contemplation of things dying that made for good tennis, not good tennis that made for our not feeling dead right now."

Dan did not respond.

"And by the way, I want to correct something." I adjusted my position on the sauna bench to face Dan. "Before we went out on the court, I think you had the impression I was depressed. I believe I was just contemplative, not depressed. You're a psychologist, Dan, you should be able to spot the difference."

Dan was now engaged. I'd challenged his profes-
sionalism. "You're right. You're not depressed. You're
grieving. I was merely using layman's jargon. You're
seeing a therapist," Dan said. "Ask him."

But Dan couldn't resist the temptation. He was a
teacher at heart, and so, while we sat—once again exceeding the suggested limit for time in a sauna—Dan
gave me a short seminar on depression and grief, dis-
tinguishing between the mood states of the depressed
person and those of the grieving person, observing
that the grieving person's moods can shift quickly
and are variable, while the depressed person usually
feels consistently depleted. The grieving person often
expresses sadness by weeping and shows anger openly
with hostility, while the depressed person often has
difficulty weeping or controlling weeping and rarely
directs anger and hostility externally. The grieving
person is usually preoccupied with the lost person or
object. The depressed person, on the other hand, is
often preoccupied with the self and has a tendency to
experience himself as worthless.

"With the aggressiveness you displayed on the
court today and the quick shift in your mood and
psychomotor activity, there's no question you're
grieving, not depressed," Dan pronounced. "You're
a textbook case. You're even absorbed with the loss
of this worthless club. A depressed person would be
preoccupied with his own worthlessness."

We were both drooping from the thick humidity of the sauna. I didn't have to suggest to Dan that we shower. We rose together. I was light-headed and balanced myself briefly at the sauna door. Dan called back to me from the showers, "As for me, I'm excited about moving out to Normandale to play. They've got terrific facilities out there. We might not have to turn the sauna into a steam room, like here, to experience some decent heat!"

Nancy, why is it that no one, not even my friend Dan, is eager to deepen into the implications of the dyings that are constantly going on in our lives? "Get some exercise," counsels Dan. "You'll snap out of it." He doesn't seem to realize that I'm exercising because I enjoy exercising. I'm not exercising to "get over" grief or to "stay healthy." He doesn't seem to realize that when I contemplate losses, including my loss of you and our loss of the court on which we've played tennis for twenty years, it is to accept our nature, not to brood. I long to have Dan understand that I'm not wallowing in grief. Understand that I'm marveling at how change is the only constant. Understand that I'm appreciating impermanence.

Nancy, you understood. I miss you.

When Dan observed that I was quiet and asked if something was "wrong with me" before we went out on the court, he was implying that there is something wrong with being quiet. There seems to be an unstated assumption that if you're OK, you must be animated. The more animated, the more OK. Even hysterical. And when I withdraw from the consensus hysteria, my friends become anxious—they conclude that I'm depressed or grieving. They want to help me out of what they see as my unfortunate predicament.

Dan isn't the only one. Just two weeks ago, my friend Ron suggested we go out to see a stand-up comic that he'd heard was hilarious. His advice was similar to Dan's.

"You need a little laughter in your life," Ron said on the phone. "You sit at home reading. You go for walks by yourself around the lake. You need to get out more."

Ron told me he'd read rave reviews about a new comedian at the Comedy Club. In town for one weekend only. Ron was sure the show would be sold out, so he'd gone ahead and ordered tickets for us without checking with me first.

"How about it?" asked Ron. "It'll be good for you."

Nancy, when did you and I last go to the Comedy Club? Ten years ago? More? I accepted Ron's invitation.

The Comedy Club hasn't changed much from when you and I were there last. Tables are crowded next to each other in the cramped pitch-black basement room. They're just large enough for drinks and

napkins to serve the four or five persons perched on
the tiny black cane chairs that are crowded up against
the tables. The small space is filled with cigarette
smoke—and a new kind of smoke that you won't
recall from when we were there last: cigar smoke.
Heavier. Thicker. Sweeter. The concentrated smoke
transported me into a different, magical world: a
Greek Orthodox Church, rich with its smells of per-
fumed incense and mysterious lighting.

The comedian was as funny as billed. I laughed—
to the point of tears on one occasion. The comic
"happened" to do a routine on death and dying.
He even tossed out the old quip about cemeteries:
"people are just *dying* to get in there, I hear." Ron
glanced over at me. I smiled back, appreciating his
concern that the comic may be a bit too "close to
the bone" for me.

He wasn't. But as the evening proceeded, I was
less able to overlook the abrasiveness of some of the
humor. The lights glared brighter. The amplification
of the comedian's voice was harsher. He seemed to
be competing with the sounds emanating from the
bar, the kitchen, and the audience. I began to withdraw. Not because of the comedian. Because of the
audience. I sensed them straining to laugh harder
and harder. I felt them grasping for more drinks,
cigarettes, cigars, and laughs. The laughter seemed
to be laced with desperation.

Am I being judgmental, Nancy? Perhaps. But the truth is that I'm no longer one of this crowd. I've lost interest in the kind of "driven" or "pushed" spontaneity that characterizes our culture. I'm much less eager to "escape" from what is happening around me. I find myself paying conscientious attention to the changes that occur constantly.

I've stopped reading the *New York Times*, the *Minneapolis StarTribune,* and the *Wall Street Journal* with the same regularity as brushing my teeth. Instead, before my first cup of Irish Breakfast tea, I read one of the daily meditation books that you kept at the bedside. I'm no longer taken by needing to know the standings of the Vikings in the Central Division of the National Football League. I'd rather go for a stroll through the bird sanctuary across from the Rose Gardens. I find myself not engaging in "small talk" because I no longer have anything "small" to talk about.

I still watch an occasional football game. I read the business section of the paper and glance over the main section. I still get together with "the guys" to play backgammon or shoot pool. But I experience these activities from a different vantage point. My sense of urgency has disappeared.

Before you died, I think I had a more defined sense of the direction in which I was headed. I knew I wanted to lawyer. I knew we wanted to travel. I knew we wanted to spend time alone together in solitude. And I knew what I had to do to move in those directions: go to law school, develop a practice that permitted us to travel, find an isolated place in northern Wisconsin that provides complete serenity. Both the goal and the path that led there were clearly articulated.

Now, each moment seems a mystery. I feel led by some ineffable force. And I'm not sure where.

When I sit down to write these letters to you, Nancy, I have no sense of what will appear on these pages. I put down a sentence. The next sentence comes to light, as if internally illumined. Sometimes I go back and tinker with a paragraph because it doesn't seem to fit with where I then find myself. But it's like I'm building a road by reverse engineering: I'm constantly at my destination, looking back to appreciate the path by which I arrived.

"Well, what did you think? Funny, wasn't he?" Ron's question jarred me back to the reality of the Comedy Club. The act had ended. The audience had given the comedian a standing ovation. Servers were rushing from table to table to settle bills.

"I particularly liked the death and dying routine," I responded. "It seems to me that we take death a bit too seriously. It was refreshing to have it treated so irreverently. It is, after all, even more a part of life than are sex and politics, the topics that comedians usually have fun with."

"You must be kidding." Ron stopped motioning for the server in order to look straight at me. "That death and dying routine was a complete 'downer.' I hated it. I don't need to pay good money to be reminded of my own mortality. I go out to have fun."

Our server came to our table. I handed him my credit card, which he added to the handful of checks and credit cards he was already holding. We would be here for a while.

"And I don't think I'm some kind of weirdo." Ron stirred the water left in his glass of Dewar's "on the rocks," the rocks in which had melted long ago. "I think that's true of most people. Everyday life's a drag. Routines are just that, routine. Folks come out on weekends to get away and escape the flatness. Welcome to life: You get up in the morning. You have breakfast. You go to work. You play a set of tennis with your buddy, Dan. You make dinner for the kids. You help the kids with homework and go to bed. Then one day, you die. That's a reality you don't need to pay some comic $30 to be reminded of."

I didn't respond until I'd asked Ron if he was looking for "feedback." He paused. He looked at me quizzically. An uncomfortable second or two of silence passed, and for a moment, I thought he might just say, "Not really." But, eventually, he said, "Of course, what's keeping you."

"What you're saying is that 'the real world' may not be all that it's cracked up to be," I said. "There's a kind of consensus frenetic hysteria that our culture labels 'normal': running hard to work during the week, then running harder during the weekend to have 'fun.' And both during the week and on the weekend, people's activities are characterized by grasping after something. Deep down, I think we all recognize that what we're grasping for isn't achievable. Maybe that's why it feels flat."

"What *is* achievable?" asked Ron.

"Experiencing what's happening right now at this very moment," I said. "But it isn't easy. It takes being quiet and paying undivided attention."

The club had cleared out. The staff was beginning to move chairs to sweep the floor. I signed the charge slip. We picked up our jackets and were outside.

The fall leaves crunched beneath our feet as we walked to the car. Though it was nearing midnight, there was a balmy softness in the air. It's what we Minnesotans call "Indian summer." The reds and yellows of the dying leaves were illumined by streetlights and the lights of passing cars. Ron kicked a small heap of leaves piled up on the sidewalk, and they danced in the air, caught by an evening zephyr.

"We're not going to have evenings like this much longer," I said.

"Yup," Ron responded. "Summer is breathing its last sigh. Beautiful, isn't it?"

Ron and I walked in silence the rest of the way to the car. I inhaled the blackness of the night. It was born within me for a moment. I exhaled. It died.

with all my love,

Dear
Nancy,

There's an image of you that I can't get out
of my mind: it's four or five months before you died;
you're being wheeled to your hospital room from the
surgical recovery room after an abdominal surgery;
a radiant glow emanates from you as you lie on the
gurney.

We spoke for only a moment, as I recall. "What
happened, dear?" I asked. "Did you have a revelation
of some kind? You look so radiant! You're beaming!
Did you have an out of body experience? Tell me
about it, Nancy."

You appeared surprised by my questions. "Nothing happened that I'm aware of. I just feel so profoundly contented. I feel completely peaceful. Did
the operation go well? Did they get everything?"

I can't remember if I even had a chance to respond
to your questions. Within moments, you had stopped
breathing. Warning buzzers on the pulse oximeter
and the vital signs monitor sounded. Nurses scurried
to your side. The surgeon and the anesthesiologist

came running. You were back on the respirator again within minutes.

While you were being intubated, for me, the room was spinning. "What happened?" I said to myself. You looked so radiant. The peaceful contentment seemed to come from somewhere deep within and permeate your entire being. And now, suddenly, you were on life support again. Your face had become gray, not the glowing reddish tinge of a moment ago. I was confused. I was frightened. Why had you suddenly stopped breathing? Were you dying? Were these to be my last moments with you? How would I survive without you?

"This happens on occasion," Dr. Wilson informed me later that day. "Anesthesia can be tricky. It can appear to have worn off, and the patient can seem to be breathing fine on her own. But there is often a residue in the system. Nancy should be fine in a couple of hours once the anesthetic gets completely out of her. Don't worry."

It wasn't a couple of hours. You remained on a respirator for almost two days. And for those days, which I measured by minutes, not hours, you could communicate with me only by writing. The legal pad at your bedside was soon filled with scribbled notes from you to me: "My mouth is SO SO SO dry," you wrote. "Ask the nurse if I can have some ice chips."

"They're coming in a minute, dear," I said out

loud after I caught myself with a pencil poised over the legal pad, drawn instinctively to respond to you in writing even though I knew that your hearing was unaffected by the tube that mechanically inflated your chest.

"How much longer does this tube have to stay in me? It is SO SO SO uncomfortable!" you scrawled.

I relayed the assurances I'd received from the doctors about the removal of the endotracheal tube. I held your hand.

"How do I look?" you asked on the yellow pad. "Should Mac still come down this afternoon? I don't want to upset him."

I assured you that you looked absolutely beautiful. I told you that I loved you with all my heart and soul. I repeated over and over that you are the love of my life. I sat by your side. And then, after the initial flurry of questions regarding medical matters and family logistics had been addressed, your handwriting became more relaxed. "Will you read to me?" you wrote in large graceful figures.

I read you your friend Susan's new book on England. I read chapter after chapter. I offered commentary contrasting our own experiences in the English countryside. But what I yearned to do was to learn more about the glow that I'd experienced emanating from you when you were first being wheeled out of the recovery room. Something significant had happened, I kept thinking. I'd never seen an expression like this on your face before. Your entire countenance had changed.

You'd not appeared at all apprehensive as you were being wheeled to the surgical prep room. I even remember noticing how the vibrant rose color of your smile contrasted with the dullness of the faded blue-and-white-striped gown you wore. You winked at me when I had to pick up my pace to walk at your side as the gurney rolled rapidly toward the *No Visitors Beyond Here* sign.

No. What I experienced when I saw you after the surgery was not relief. It was a deeper transformation of some kind. I even remember commenting to you that you looked to me like someone who had seen an apparition. "Did you see the face of God or something?" I recall asking you.

"I adore you," you wrote on the legal pad without replying to my question.

At a family gathering last week at my parents' cabin, I commented to your sister Jane that after your abdominal surgery, you looked like someone who'd seen the face of God. "I think I've never seen such a beatific expression on someone's face," I said to Jane.

"No one can see the face of God," Jane declared emphatically as she skipped a stone across the still lake. We both watched the stone dribble in smaller and smaller hops and then disappear into the water.

The wind had died down with the setting sun. Soft clouds began to cover the sky. I could easily have commented on the majesty of my parents' lake cabin. Instead, I found myself explaining to Jane that when I spoke of seeing the face of God, I was speaking metaphorically, not literally. And then I went on to lecture—Nancy, I acknowledge that it may have been in a somewhat condescending tone—that I did not see God as a "stern father" who glowers at his children. I rattled on about the divine presence as transcendent. I'm embarrassed to say that I may have even made an unsolicited observation to Jane about "mature" religious beliefs, an unveiled jab at what I see as Jane's religious fundamentalism.

"I know you didn't mean that Nancy literally saw the face of a person called God," responded Jane, apparently unaffected. "What I was saying is that humans cannot witness the true majesty of God. Mortals are allowed to see only glimpses of God's goodness through moments of grace. We can't see God straight on. It says so right in the Bible."

I should have let the matter drop. I know from experience that it's a mistake to get into a debate with Jane about what the Bible does or does not say. Jane seems to be able to quote appropriate verses from memory without effort. But that evening, she didn't have to rely on memory. Jane had a miniature copy of the Bible with her in her purse. She pulled it out and turned quickly to Exodus 33 in the Older Testament:

> *Jehovah says to Moses "Thou canst not see my face; for man shall not see me and live." And Jehovah said, "Behold, there is a place by me, and thou shalt stand upon the rock: and it shall come to pass, while my glory passeth by, that I will put thee in a cleft of the rock, and will cover thee with my hand until I have passed by: And I will take away my hand, and thou shalt see my back; but my face shall not be seen."*

"So. You get the picture? Nancy *can't* have seen the face of God," Jane announced as she put the Bible back in her purse. "No one is permitted to. Not even Moses."

I did "get the picture" in that I had used the expression "See the face of God" thoughtlessly. Still, I wanted to be alone with the implications of what Jane had said: "For humans shall not experience the glory of the transcendental first hand—*and live*." Had you seen something that mortals are not permitted to see?

"You're probably right," I said to Jane as I started down the hill by myself toward the lake. "The majesty of the true nature of the divine is probably too over-whelming for anyone to comprehend." I said I'd catch up with her later, after my walk.

It was now dark. The clouds toyed with the light of the moon, creating a scrim through which the moon's outline was mysteriously diffuse. Its dispersed light softened the path on the unlit trail. Then, at once, the curtains were dramatically pulled back to reveal the full majesty of nocturnal illumination. The moon's focused beam reflected on the lake and mir-rored its penetrating glow. And in the blackness of the still water, the reflection of the moon appeared more moonlike than its image in the sky. It was al-most as if the moon had left its body and was ema-nating from deep within the lake.

"Nancy, did you see more than a glimpse of glory during your surgery?" I asked as I walked along the moonlit path. "Did you discover what you *are*, not just what you are *not*?"

"What *are* you, Nancy?" I questioned aloud in the empty night air as I continued to stare at the moon—glowing from within the lake and appearing more tangible than its body in the heavens above.

"I am you," a familiar soft voice replied.

I was startled. I quickly turned to assure myself that there was not another person that had come up behind me on the isolated path to the lake.

Nobody was there. I sighed a deep sigh of resignation.

"I am the sigh within the sigh," the voice continued.

The late night air had become cold. I picked up my stride and headed up the hill.

"I thought I heard voices," Jane said to me as I came up the path. "Is somebody out there?"

I paused.

"No. Nothing that thou canst see," I replied.

with all my love,

*Dear
Nancy,*

     This morning I searched again for an au-
diotape from you to me. Might it have been stuck
among some of your papers in your study? Did it
fall in the crack between the mattress and the head-
board? Was it in the drawer of the nightstand that I
had searched so many times before, hidden in some
dark back corner that I had overlooked? I looked
in all of those places. I looked in others. Nothing.
Where would you put something that you might
want me to discover later, after your death?

     I had cajoled you about making an audiotape for
me. "Why won't you make me a tape like the ones
you're making for Julia and Mac? Am I not as important as they?" I pleaded.

     "You already know everything I have to say to
you," I recall you responding. "I've said it all to you,
and I've said it over and over: I love you. I love you
with all my heart. I will always love you. That's all
that matters. The worldview stuff, the principles that
I want to remind Julia and Mac of—you know them,

you and I've talked about them all of our lives. Our worldviews were formed together. They were developed and refined by our minds and souls rubbing against each other for over forty years. I wouldn't know what to say in a tape for you—you'd be hearing me say back to you all of your own views. Andy, we are soul mates. A tape for you coming from my head or heart almost feels demeaning."

"I might just appreciate hearing your voice," I persisted. "I don't mind that there is nothing new. Say the same things again."

I knew as I talked that I had not convinced you. Why, now, five months after your death, should I expect that you might have changed your mind and left a tape hidden somewhere for me? Why now do I find myself desperately searching through unlikely cracks and crevices looking for something that, in my heart, I know does not exist?

I remember when the audiotapes were first mentioned. It was months before you died. "Do any of these tape recorders have microphones?" you asked. "It looks to me like all these portable tape recorders we have are just for playing tapes, not for recording. Why do they call them tape *recorders* if they don't record?"

"The stereo system downstairs has a plug-in microphone, and I think Mac's boom box has one built in," I offered. "Wouldn't they work?"

"No. I'm looking for something really portable. Something I can just clip on and use while I'm walking around or lying down in bed. I think it might be easier for me just to put some of the things I want to say on tape. My worldview is scattered through my writings, and they aren't that accessible. The ones that have been published were intended for a larger audience. What I want to do is to bring my views down to the practical personal level for some people, especially, Julia and Mac.

"I don't mean I feel at all like I'm going to die—not anytime soon in any event. I just thought that it would be a good thing to do. You never know what might happen. I'd want you to keep them and give them to Julia and Mac at the right time. Kids are so vulnerable today. Their views are so influenced by mass culture and the media. If I'm not around, I'd like them to be able to hear my voice—to have something that will ground them when they feel at sea."

As I rummaged through the drawers of your desk, I ran across a sheet of paper entitled *Guiding Principles.* It contained notes in your handwriting, implying that the *Principles* would form the basis for a spirituality manual. Nancy, I didn't know that you were in the process of thinking about a manual to complement your work as a spiritual director. I started to read the principles. Here's what I read:

- *What we think and feel interiorly, manifests exteriorly (we create our reality).*
- *Everything that happens to us is our teacher (synchronicity).*
- *Everything we do comes back to us 100 percent (we create our karma every minute of our lives— every good and bad thought, word and deed comes back to us).*
- *To change our lives, we must first change our thoughts.*
- *To change our thoughts, we must first be aware of what we are thinking.*
- *To be aware of what we are thinking, we must meditate—take time for our thoughts to slow down—only then can we be aware of them. We then begin to discern our "script"—our way of approaching life that was imprinted upon us at a precognitive stage, which is our "automatic pilot." With regular meditation, new ways of reacting and acting start "occurring" to us, especially ways that are kind, merciful, nonjudgmental—we begin to take on the mind of God and start to see things/people/acts with unconditional compassion.*
- *When we meditate, we are not governed by the law of matching energy (negativity is matched with negativity, anger with anger, aggression*

> *with aggression), and we are able to meet nega-*
> *tivity with nonresistance and kindness, changing*
> *the negative person and the world.*
> - *No one can harm you or benefit you, unless you*
>   *allow it.*

I realized, Nancy, that though I may know these principles, since you died, I've not been practicing them. I've fallen out of a daily meditation practice. I know, intellectually, that my day always unfolds more gracefully when I meditate—that things take less time and unimagined doors open, permitting me to accomplish things with ease—but I have allowed myself to become convinced that there are too many demands on my time. I could give myself an extra twenty minutes each day by not meditating, my brain says to me as the alarm goes off. And the call of the bed is so attractive in the morning. That extra twenty minutes of sleep seems like the gift of an extra hour. I was eager to know what you had said in your tapes to Julia and Mac.

"You know the tape Mom made for you, Mac," I said that evening at dinner. "I was wondering if you would let me hear it. I know Mom made it just for you. And it is yours to keep private just between you and Mom, if that's what you want. I can understand that and I respect that. I know you listen to it by yourself in your room. You may want to keep it

your special private thing. That's perfectly OK with
me. But I miss Mom a lot. And if you don't mind,
I think I might be comforted by hearing her words
to you."

"You've never heard the tape, Dad?" Mac asked
with genuine surprise. "But you're the one who gave
it to me. Didn't you listen to it?"

"No. Mom gave it to me to give to you. She
didn't say for me *not* to listen to it. But I thought it
was kind of like a letter addressed to you—I wouldn't
be comfortable opening your personal mail either."

Mac went to his room to get the tape. He handed
to me. "Don't wreck it, Dad. It's really special."

That evening, after Mac had gone to sleep, I made
myself a cup of tea—Earl Grey fully caffeinated tea,
despite the late hour. I sat down by myself in my
study in the large overstuffed leather chair with a box
of tissues, having learned from my grief group that
having them handy is practical planning. I was apprehensive about hearing your voice again after this long
time. I was eager to learn how you would personalize
the "perennial wisdom" for a fourteen-year-old boy.

The tape was filled with a different kind of wisdom: affirmations of Mac being a "golden child,"
examples of the joy he has given you, his many accomplishments that delighted you, the direction that
you see him taking in his life. Gentle. Caring. No
deathbed instructions about how to live his life. No

rules and regulations. No advice about meditating. No "perennial wisdom." Just an affirmation of your love. Just an affirmation of Mac's importance as a child of God. Just an affirmation that his life and all lives are a bountiful cornucopia of the fruit of rich experiences.

Uncomplicated. Validating. I'd been looking for something too complex. Nancy, your tape *was* the personalization of the "perennial wisdom," wasn't it?

With all the caffeine I had just had, I decided to stay up a while longer. And meditate.

with all my love,

PATIENCE

from *Gifts of Spirit;* chapel meditation,
March 14, 1993

. . . We don't meet God in heaven. We meet God here every minute of our lives and we do not recognize God. Unless we are in heaven here, chances are, we won't be in heaven over there. . . . Luckily, there is a spiritual methodology of how to wake up to the dimension in which the ordinary is more than enough.

One important means to waking up is the spiritual practice of patience. Did you expect a spiritual practice that is more exciting? A lot of people associate patience with passivity or powerlessness. It could seem that patience is an oppressive word used by the powerful to get the powerless under control.

But true patience is the opposite of a passive waiting in which we let things happen and allow others to make decisions. Patience means to enter actively into the thick of life and to fully bear the suffering within and around us. Patience involves the capacity to taste, smell, touch, hear, and see as fully as possible the inner and outer events of our lives; to enter our lives with open ears, eyes, and hands so that we really know what is going on.

The root of the word *patience* is in the Latin word *pati,* which means suffering. So, to be patient requires a great deal of courage. When a sensitive subject comes up, when a painful memory occurs, instead of changing the subject or fleeing the memory, patience helps us go against the grain of our impulse of fight or flight and helps us to stay with the memory, to suffer the pain, to listen carefully to what presents itself, to live it through. . . .

Patience opens us to the "something more" dimension of time. When we are impatient, we experience the present moment as useless, meaningless. . . . Impatience makes us live by clock time—I want to hurry up and get my degree, get married, get the new job—maybe then I'll find the meaning of life and be happy.

In contrast, during patient moments, we feel the present moment as full, rich, meaningful. Somehow we know that in this moment—all is contained—the searching and the finding, the sorrow and the joy, the expectation and the realization. Our present moment may not be necessarily happy but in this present moment, we feel real life has touched us.

Dear
Nancy,

    I've been thinking about your *Guiding Principles,* particularly the principle about synchronicity—"*everything* that happens to us is our teacher." While practicing piano with Mac last week, I realized that your absence as Mac's piano coach has been a teacher for me.

    I know how important you felt Mac's piano playing was for his cognitive development, and I've had every intention to continue your discipline of sitting with him every day. Nancy, I'm sorry. For me, the day somehow seems to slip away. Mac comes home late from floor hockey practice, I make dinner, I help him with his homework, I clean up, and then it's time for Mac to go to bed. Practicing piano with Mac seems to end up last on an endless list of things to do.

    Mac's weekly piano lesson was coming up, and I suddenly realized that I hadn't practiced with him even once. That week Mrs. Reed had given Mac more than just phonic Suzuki pieces to practice from memory. For the first time, she had started teaching

Mac to read music. I sat down with Mac at the piano to go through the assignment. He couldn't identify the name of a single note on the homework page that Mrs. Reed had left with him to complete.

I reviewed with Mac the mnemonic devices that you and I learned as kids—"F-A-C-E" for the spaces of the treble clef, "*Every Good Boy Does Fine*" for the lines. "It's a lot to remember all at once," I said to Mac. "That's why it helps to have something like a jingle to remember the names of each line and space." I suggested we go slow. We would start with just one line—the bottom line. "What's the bottom line called?" I asked.

"A," responded Mac.

"The bottom *line*, Mac. Remember? The lines are named 'Every Good Boy Does Fine,' right? Which is the first letter of the *first* word in the rhyme?"

"C," responded Mac.

"Mac, are you concentrating?" My voice started to become strained and louder. "The *spaces* are F-A-C-E. Right? C is a space, not a line. Do you get that? The first *line* is E—it is the first line on the bottom of the treble clef, and it is the first letter of the first word of *Every Good Boy Does Fine*." I hammered the clef with my finger and repeated each word in the homonym with staccato emphasis. "The bottom line is E, not C. Can you remember that?"

"Y-y-yup."

"What is this note?" I pointed to a note on the bottom line.

"F," responded Mac.

I could see that Mac was feeling under pressure and that the tension was escalating. Yet I couldn't stop myself. I heard myself gritting through my teeth, "No. No. No. *Not* F. That note is E. The bottom line is E. Don't you even know the difference between a line and a space?

"What is this?" I embedded my fingernail in a line on the clef. "Is it a line or a space?"

"Space," responded Mac.

Mac moved away from me on the piano bench, and I could see Mac's self-esteem shrink. But an automatic response sequence had been triggered, and I heard myself shrieking, "Come on, Mac. Concentrate. Pay attention. Let's get it right!"

Mac started to cry. Only then did I start to apprehend that I was responding to something deeper than the frustration of teaching abstract concepts to a person with Down syndrome. Why? I asked myself silently. Why am I taking this so seriously? I flashed back to my own childhood.

When my parents still lived on Irving, we had a dark brown Cable grand. It had scrolled legs like gnarled tree trunks and an elaborate garland carved on the side of the soundboard. It sat in the sunroom, off my father's study. The full-sized antique piano seemed to take up the entire room. The tropical plants and wicker chairs that I felt rightfully belonged in a sunroom appeared to be dwarfed by a monstrosity that crowded out everything else. Why couldn't we just have a hi-fi like other people? I remember wondering. And why did I have to take piano lessons instead of going to football practice? None of the other kids in junior high had to rush home for piano lessons.

The piano took up just as much space in my life as it did in the sunroom. It crowded out the activities that I felt rightfully belonged there—tossing a ball with my father, watching TV.

We had no TV. "Nothing worthwhile to watch on TV," my father would pronounce. "It's just a waste of time. There aren't enough hours in a lifetime to even read the classics. Maybe we'll get a television set if they figure out how to make the picture sharper or they ever come out with color. It's bad for your eyes."

In the late 1950s, color technology arrived. But we still didn't get a TV. I now wonder if at that point it would have mattered. The script had been written and imprinted in me: life is serious; there's not enough time to get even the important things done.

I guess tossing a ball fell into the same philosophical worldview—not serious enough. And ball playing was risky. My hands might become hardened.

My fingertips roughened. I might break a finger and miss a couple of weeks of lessons, not to mention the practice time. My career as a prospective concert pianist would be jeopardized. "Do you think Van Cliburn is out tossing a ball around?" my father would ask.

"But I'm not going to become a professional pianist."

"You never know," my father would assert. "And it's not a question of whether or not you become a concert pianist. Why would you want to make a half-hearted attempt at *anything*? If it's worth doing, it's worth doing well. Some day you'll thank me."

I never did thank my father for not having played ball with me or for learning to take life seriously. But just before he died, I did thank him for sitting with me at the piano.

"You spent a lot of time with me at the piano, Dad," I recall saying to him long after he'd retired and had his second stroke. "I appreciate it." I told him it wasn't until I was in my mid-thirties that I realized what a gift he'd given me. That I understood the joy that comes from making one's own music—even though I'd lost much of my technical proficiency.

"You could have been good, really good," my father responded. "You've got the fingers of a pianist. I pushed you. If only you had concentrated and practiced . . . you'd have accomplished something lasting. You gave up. You quit."

I didn't reply. I couldn't articulate what I didn't then comprehend. I never said anything about my sadness at our not having played ball together. Anything about my anger at being different from the other kids. Anything about seriousness having become my script. Nancy, I now wonder if, but for your absence, I'd still not have discerned the roots of my seriousness because you would have sat at the piano with Mac. I would still be observing, listening, without an opportunity for my impatience to be my teacher.

After my blowup, I explained to Mac that at that moment I had relived sitting at the piano bench with my father. It was scary, I said. I apologized to Mac and asked if he, too, was scared.

"My father pushed me hard. I'm not sure he knew how it distanced him from me. Did you know, Mac, that I never once in my life played 'catch' with my dad? I'm not sure he knew how pushing me to excel, instead of just playing a game, made me resent him. Do you feel like pushing me away when I demand that you get it right?"

"I just know it was more f-f-fun with Mom," Mac replied. "She was tough. She made me practice hard. But it was like a game."

"Would you like to quit?" I asked. "There's nothing that says that you've got to take piano lessons."

"I love piano," he replied. "And I *want* to get better. Mom told me in her tape that piano made her happy. It still makes her happy. It makes *me* happy. I just don't want it to be so s-s-s-serious."

"Should we take a break?" I asked. "Do you want to shoot some baskets with me before it gets dark?"

"Yeah. And be prepared to lose, Dad," Mac said with mock seriousness. "But first let's finish with these notes. This note, here, on this line is E, right?" said Mac as he pointed to the correct note. "And the one just above it, in the space, that's F, isn't it?" he added.

with all my love,

*Dear
Nancy,*

I hadn't seen Sheldon since your memorial service, and when I happened to be seated next to him on a flight to Chicago last week, there was a lot of catching up to do. Well into the conversation, I referred to you as "my wife." Suddenly, his eyes left mine, and I noticed him glance down at my left hand. Your wedding band was on my fourth finger, as it has been night and day for thirty years. Sheldon looked back up at me. "When did you get married?" he asked, his confusion evident in the hesitancy with which he spoke. "Hasn't it been only a few months since Nancy died?"

Shelly and I are not close friends. I don't discuss my worldviews with him. I doubt if we've ever had a conversation about our feelings or about our philosophies of life. I didn't sense that now was the right time to start by launching into an explanation of how I continue to wear your wedding band because I feel that you will *always* be my wife, just as Shakespeare will *always* be The Bard, no matter how many bards follow him in the annals of literature. An explanation of how I continue to wear your wedding band because removing your wedding band would be like removing my fingerprint. I would have had to distinguish for Sheldon between clinging to your memory and knowing that you and I will be always connected as mates, regardless of circumstances, including the circumstance of your death. I looked for ways to divert the question.

As I searched my mind for possible responses, I was reminded of the trick that your mother delighted in playing at cocktail parties. With an entirely flat affect, she would introduce your father as her "first" husband. The unsuspecting guests would be momentarily at a loss for words. What's she doing here with her *first* husband? Are she and her *current* husband separated? Does her current husband know that she is out with a former husband? What kind of "open" relationship does this conservative blue-blooded matron have with the men in her life?

Your mother was careful not to step over the line and actually misstate the truth. If she was cornered, she'd explain. Your father was her first and *only* husband. He was first and always would be. Even after fifty years of marriage, she still swooned when he came into the room.

I, too, still swoon. You don't have to come into the room. I swoon just thinking of you. You were my soul mate. You were my friend. You were my wife. Your death has not changed any of that. You *are* my wife.

I decided to use your mother's approach. "Yes, I did get married," I said to Shelly with an entirely flat affect. "I married a girl I met in third grade. We were childhood sweethearts."

"How wonderful for you," Shelly beamed. "Connecting again with someone from grade school. You must have been meant for each other. Mazel tov. May you live a long, happy life together. What's her name?"

"Her name is Nancy," I replied.

with all my love,

Dear
Nancy,

Mac has a new softball coach. His name
is David. Nancy, you'd like him.

Dave's a massive man—near three hundred
pounds, I suspect, and a good six foot two. He's
got a bit of a belly. But he doesn't look overweight.
Just big. His physique overwhelms his soft face and
gentle eyes.

David was the director of an inclusive high
school program in Toronto. He authored Quebec's
legislation for the integration of disabled persons
in public schools. He was an education professor at
the "U of M" for ten years and has been involved in
many of your favorite causes. I'm surprised we'd not
met him before.

Although he's had no prior experience coach-
ing, David loves baseball. He's taken to coordinating
adaptive softball in Richfield with a passion. Being
sensitive to possible needs for persons with disabilities, he asked Mac and me to meet with him to talk
about Mac's background and his goals.

We spent little time talking baseball. David wanted to hear about growing up with Down syndrome. About parenting a child with special needs. We talked for almost half an hour about inclusion, isolation, the exhaustion involved in constantly breaking new ground, the need for a cheerleader—all the things you, Nancy, handled so well. I spoke about the crucial role you played in empowering Mac's teachers and the vacuum we feel without your guidance.

David told us the softball team would be equally balanced between "typical" kids and ones with special needs, pointing out that we all become more fully human through inclusive interaction, a view that I had not heard articulated in quite this way since you died. I could almost hear your familiar feminine voice emanating from Dave's huge masculine body, eloquently expressing the benefits of inclusion and the lessons we learn from one another by being exposed to situations that are not comfortable. I felt an instantaneous kinship with David.

As I was getting up to leave, David mentioned that the bleeding had stopped. "Bleeding?" I asked. "What bleeding?"

"Oh, I thought you knew," David replied. "I've got cancer. It's in remission. But I've had most of my right breast removed. The incision from the last surgery opened up again a couple of weeks ago."

"You've had a mastectomy?" I asked. "I didn't know men have mastectomies."

While talking, we sauntered over to a park bench overlooking the softball field and sat down. The two elms that cuddled the bench were not yet full enough to block the sun. David glanced straight up at the bright sunlight and handed me a baseball cap.

"Men do have mastectomies. I've had three breast surgeries. They're called lumpectomies." David told me he constantly lives with the prospect of more treatment. Like you, Nancy, David has had chemotherapy. In addition he's undergone radiation treatments.

"It's a strange paradox: it takes having been close to death in order to be fully open to life," David said.

I thought it a strange paradox that our conversation had turned deep so quickly. I'd met this man only an hour ago, and we were now talking about death and worldviews. Who was this man? I wondered. I glanced over at Mac and his friend Wayne. They were barely visible at the far end of the park.

"I used to be frightened by the prospect of dying," David continued. "I so desperately wanted to stay alive. I felt I had so much work left to do. When I was first diagnosed fifteen years ago, I was still in graduate school, just months from finishing my dissertation. My research on total inclusion in

the education of persons with disabilities had just
barely scratched the surface. Most of the information was anecdotal. I was convinced it needed to be
approached scientifically. No one had systematically
studied inclusion in the United States. No one was
really looking at the societal and cultural components. I couldn't believe that this work that I felt
so much passion about would go unfinished.

"But mostly, I felt this overpowering sense of
urgency. I was desperate to stay alive. I was desperate to do what I thought was my life's work. I
couldn't understand how something like this could
happen to somebody at such a young age. It just
wasn't right that I should die now. I needed to live
to finish this work."

I was riveted by David's story. Elements of it were
so much like my own response to my diagnosis of
coccidioidal meningitis when I was thirty-seven.

"Somewhere deep within my soul, I knew that
what I needed was to learn to 'let go.' I needed to
surrender to God's will and ease up a bit. Stop struggling. I needed to let go of my ego's investment in
inclusive education. I spoke of being 'called' to do
this work, but in reality, I had to acknowledge that
I was pushing and forcing, not allowing myself to be
led. I was sure *I* knew the way. A small voice inside
me was screaming in protest at becoming a follower
instead of the guide. I knew my life and the little

voice inside me were in conflict, but I couldn't let go. I didn't know how. I only knew how to tenaciously cling to my life.

"Now, in retrospect, I realize that living had never really been a genuine *choice* for me. By clinging to life, I couldn't *choose* it. Interesting, isn't it, that when you don't have the choice *not* to have something, you don't really have the choice *to* have it, either. I was miserable. I bemoaned my fate. I argued with the doctors. I harangued."

David stopped. "This is becoming a long story," he said and asked if I had the time or was really interested in hearing him philosophize about the meaning of life. "Today's not Sunday," he joked.

I leaned forward and clasped my knees to my chest, absorbed by this giant of a man and his story. David went on.

"During my second surgery, the desperate energy around staying alive suddenly lost its hold on me. It was as if a lightbulb had been turned on. All of a sudden I saw life differently. I still wanted to live. But it wasn't mine to try to possess. I saw it as a gift that was on loan to me. I realized I had all my energy tied up in clinging instead of being grateful for the gift. I was clinging to all those 'shoulds' about what I had to accomplish in life and what contributions I needed to make to justify my existence on this planet. But by clinging to life, I realize that I was in fact smothering my life. I was holding on to life so hard that I was choking it. I now realize that I had never made a choice to live. Instead, I had a strong-hold on life."

I could visualize Dave's massive body pinning down "life" in a half-nelson wrestling hold. There would be no escaping Dave's powerful grip.

"Now that I've eased up on my hold just a bit, it seems I'm getting much more done—and I'm enjoy-ing it too. I wake up every morning and feel blessed by the miracle of being alive. I look around my room and marvel at all of the wonderful books on my book-shelf that I've had the privilege to read—and all the books whose words patiently wait to have their pages opened and read. I go into the kitchen, make a bowl of oatmeal for breakfast, and see in its rich texture a connection to the entire universe—the sun, the rain, the minerals in the earth. It's all there, a cornucopia set before me to marvel at, appreciate, be nourished by, and enjoy."

"Oatmeal?" I looked at David quizzically.

"Initially, when I looked at my oatmeal, I think all I saw was food," David explained. "Health food at that—something you ate because it was good for you, not because it was enjoyable. As time passed, I began to see more deeply—I saw textures and components—the grain, the oats, sugar, raisins, the difference between flat-cut and steel-cut oats. I actually experienced the nutritive benefits in it. And it started to taste different. It was no longer just break-fast food."

I nodded. I was beginning to understand.

"Then I began to see even more deeply—I saw deeper textures and components of the oatmeal—the farmer, the farmer's grandfather. You know, when you think about it, there is nothing that is just 'oat-meal' in and of itself. 'Oatmeal' consists entirely of 'non-oatmeal' elements. In reality 'oatmeal' is just a verbal construct that we have developed to describe this combination of 'non-oatmeal' components."

I'd never considered oatmeal as made up of any-thing other than grains and water. But I couldn't dispute that but for the sun, the rain, and the farmer, there would be no oatmeal.

"I was not appreciative of oatmeal, or of life for that matter, until I got my disease." David's face glis-tened in the sunlight below the rim of his baseball cap. "I took both for granted. Now, I can't imagine having lived the rest of my life being the person I was before I became sick. I suppose I would have completed my dissertation with lots of documenta-tion and scholarly analysis of the 'right' way to edu-cate disabled persons. But I know I wouldn't have connected to the people I was studying. I probably would have continued to take them for granted like I had taken the oatmeal for granted. I suspect oatmeal would have continued to nourish my body, and I suspect my academic work would have continued to nourish my mind. But would either have nourished my soul?"

David paused. "It would certainly never have occurred to me to coach softball to develop a relationship with the kids I was researching. Life would have continued to be a spectator sport for me.

"But enough about the 'Zen of Oatmeal,'" David chuckled. "Seems you and Mac have an appreciation of the interconnectedness of it all. How'd you come to wake up?"

"I'm not sure we have," I replied. I confessed to David that we miss you a lot, Nancy. That sometimes I feel like we cling to your memory in the same smothering way David described his first bout with cancer. That because your physical body is no longer here, it's easy to see you as separate from us and harder for us to experience you in the same way David described experiencing the farmer's grandfather as contained in, and making up, the oatmeal.

Yet I remember times when I experienced you as made up of "non-Nancy" elements. When you said something I knew came directly out of the mouth of your favorite drama coach. When you made a gesture that was identical to your father's. I suppose David was suggesting that we could connect to those same experiences of you now. If, as with the oatmeal, you

are made up entirely of "non-Nancy" elements, most
of those elements are still as much around today as
they were a year and a half ago.

Wayne had left for home, and Mac was approaching us. He mechanically pounded his fist into his
baseball glove.

"I'm so sorry about the death of your mother,"
David said to Mac. "Being out in the park in the
summertime might be a good way to connect with
her. I'm really looking forward to having you on
the team."

David turned his head and nodded, tipping his
head forward at an angle and dipping his chin just
like you do, Nancy. Both Mac and I were speechless
for a moment. We'd not seen this gesture for over
a year. It was unique to you. We used to tease you
about it—your "signature" gesture.

Mac gave David a long hug, barely able to reach
his arms around Dave's girth. I predict we'll have a
terrific softball season.

with all my love,

Dear
Nancy,

Our wilderness retreat has undergone its
semiannual transformation. The skeletal bones of
fallen trees are no longer visible. The birch on the
hillside across the lake no longer look like colossal
bristles on a hedgehog's back. The underbrush has
created a thick living wall, penetrable by the gopher,
the squirrel, and even the deer. Not, however, by the
human eye. The woods are solid green.

Yet the window boxes on our deck remain lifeless.
What were pink geraniums and rose hypoestes last
summer are shriveled on lifeless stems. The tiny leaves
of the silverthorn are ashen. They're a reminder that
not all growth is perennial. These window-box plants
were meant to live one year only.

Your absence accentuates the roles you and I as-
signed to ourselves. Did we consciously agree that
you would go to Northwoods Nursery and choose
plants for the window boxes while I cleared trails
in the woods? I don't recall our ever having talked
about it. It just seemed to happen automatically: one

weekend each spring, you'd announce that you were
going to the nursery in Hayward. You'd come back
with a car trunk exploding with colors—pinks, yellows, reds. On occasion you'd ask me to help dig out
the dead plants or spread compost. I, on occasion,
would ask you to assist with a tree fallen over a trail.
But it was unquestioned that you were in charge of
the window boxes and the plantings along the walkway; I was in charge of the woods.

Dana and my mother will arrive tomorrow.
They won't permit the window boxes to remain un-
tended. The gray shriveled remains will be replaced
with bright colored flowers. Until then, I sit staring
at these reminders of you and of the separate roles
we played.

When my mother and Dana arrive, they do take
control. "Dana and I'll just run into town and pick
up some plants for these window boxes," my mother
announces. "Looks like geraniums and hypoestes
were planted here last. We'll do the same again. OK?"

If I'm to participate, I know I'd better speak up
quickly. I point out that in all the summers you and
I've spent here, I've never actually been inside the
Northwoods Nursery. That I've talked to the owner,
Barb, on the phone, and that I met her once when
she was here to consult with you about landscaping.
That I think it's time for me to do more than observe
the finished product. "I'd like to come along," I said.

"Oh, but you were up late, son, and, besides, you've already got so much on your plate. You should take a rest," my mother replied with the same authoritative tone she used when I was a child living at home. "Dana and I've planted so many gardens, dear. It won't take us but a minute."

My mother's demeanor indicated that this is a serious mission and that they'd be hampered by the presence of a non-gardener. But I insisted. My mother reluctantly gestured for me to join them.

As we entered the nursery, Barbara hurried over to welcome us. "I'm sorry about your wife, Nancy," she said. "Nancy's ability to connect with people was unique. Even though I saw her only once a year, I felt she truly cared about me and about what was going on in my life. She was a friend, not a customer. With Hayward being a town of only 1,900, you'd expect we'd be close with all of our regular customers. But, in fact, it's rare that I connect with someone at a deep level. Nancy was one of a kind. I miss her a lot. It must be very hard for you."

"Yes, it is," I responded. "I could never have imagined the subtle ways in which I'd miss her." I commented that we'd inadvertently adopted an understanding that you were in charge of the annuals and I was in charge of the perennials. That I know nothing about the annuals. That I'll have to learn all that. "For example, do you know what kind of fertilizer Nancy used?" I asked.

"Well, for one thing, Nancy never used much chemical fertilizer," Barbara answered. "I'm sure she composted. That's the best fertilizer there is, you know." She explained that since we're not around that often, it's a good idea to stay away from chemical fertilizers. That with chemicals we'd run the risk of burnout since we can't count on consistent watering. And Barbara didn't have to go back to her records to tell us what varieties of plants you customarily selected. Though they'd change from year to year, she knew them by heart.

Barbara's inventory was spread through three greenhouses. We stopped to marvel at the sugar daddy petunias. We assessed how they would look next to the bright yellow marigolds, which were located in a separate building. Dana recalled the year that you had scarlet dianthus along the entire length of the border of the walk.

When the trunk to the car was rich with colors and we were ready to go, Barbara approached me. "I've been reflecting on what you said about annuals and perennials," she said. "You know the distinction is really a bit illusory. Perennials don't last indefinitely. Not even the largest of plants, the redwood and sequoia trees, last forever." She explained that "perennials" eventually end up in the same place as "annuals"—in the compost heap. They decompose right in the forest. Carpenter ants and insects slowly take them apart, and their decomposed remains feed the next growth of trees, just like the decomposed plants in the compost heap feed the geraniums and coleus that my mother, Dana, and I would plant that afternoon. "The organism that's alive is not the 'annual' plant or the 'perennial' tree," she said. "It's the ecosystem itself."

Barbara went on to say that it would be more accurate to refer to both the "annuals" and the "perennials" as "cyclicals." They're around in one form for a cycle. Then they're around in another form for another cycle. They're compost for awhile, then they're trees or plants for awhile. But their life doesn't end with the end of a cycle.

As we left, Barbara handed us a couple of castle mix celosia plants. "Nancy would have loved these, they're so whimsical," said Barbara. "Please take them. They're my gift to Nancy's walkway."

We thanked her and headed back to our wilderness retreat. "It's a bit different going to a small-town nursery," commented Dana. "I can see why Nancy and Barbara got along so well. Barb sure seems to have a larger view of things. I'm fascinated by what she had to say about the similarity between annuals and perennials."

I recalled that you, too, felt at peace with the natural cycles of life and death. That you, too, would have seen dead plants in the compost heap not as dead, but as a cycle that the flower goes through.

We dug up the "dead" hypoestes and geraniums from the window boxes and placed them in the compost heap. With bare hands, I formed a hole for the new "living" plants and then filled it with loam from the compost heap. The soil felt cool and damp on my hands.

My work gloves had become heavy with the moisture. "The texture of the compost heap is remarkably moist," I observed to my mother. The old brown and gray plants start out papery light. But in the process of dying, they've become thick, juicy, and dark black. "I was just thinking that the compost even *feels* alive."

"What doesn't feel alive if you let yourself get intimate with it?" I noticed my mother had long ago removed her gardening gloves and was working the soil with her bare hands.

with all my love,

Dear
   Nancy,

Today is August 9th. Your birthday.

Nancy, you loved to celebrate. To celebrate almost anything. And birthdays were occasions that gave you an excuse to celebrate without provoking a possible barb from me.

"Won't Sally be embarrassed to receive a dozen roses just because she called to apologize to her mother?" I recall cross-examining you. "Nancy, it's routine for adult children to get into a fight with a parent and then make up. Aren't you making a bit of a big deal out of this? I'd be embarrassed if someone sent me flowers to celebrate my having talked to my mother."

"You aren't Sally," you'd respond. "This has been a major blockage in Sally's life. It's caused her a lot of distress. She was very hurt. It took a lot of courage on her part to make that call to her mother. I want to acknowledge her courage and self-confidence. And, in any event, you don't need a *reason* to send someone flowers. Having had the courage to call her mother just gives me something to mention in the card. There's absolutely no doubt that Sally will appreciate the flowers. They are coming from my heart. People get embarrassed only if they sense that what you're doing isn't genuine."

My reproaches to what I viewed as excessiveness did not deter you. You sent a dozen roses to celebrate a new puppy, another for a minor promotion, a finished grant application, the last day of exams—before the grades even came out.

Today I wish I could be excessive. I'd gladly have bought Mac twelve dozen roses. But Mac and I are at an isolated retreat center in Colorado, attending a conference on inclusion for people with disabilities. Julia is in Peru. Tomorrow she'll depart to hike the Inca Trail. I've made arrangements with Julia for her to call our hotel this evening from Cuzco so that Julia, Mac, and I can connect on your special day.

The phone rings. I eagerly reach to pick it up. But it's only a new friend Mac has made in the conference. "Tell him you'll call him back," I say to Mac. "Julia is supposed to be calling any minute. We don't want to miss her call." Mac methodically makes arrangements to meet his new friend to shoot pool without displaying any noticeable hurry. What's the big deal, I can visualize him saying to himself. How many times has my sister made *me* wait?

Mac finally gets off the phone. I call the front

desk to ask if any calls have come in while the line was busy and ask that we be interrupted if we happen to be using the phone when Julia calls. "I'm expecting a call from my daughter from a small village in South America," I say to the attendant at the front desk. "It may be difficult for her to get to a phone or to place a call, and we don't want to miss it."

The attendant explains that the hotel doesn't have the technology to be able to interrupt a call in a guest's room or to let us know that there is another call holding. "Just stay off the phone," he counsels. We sit. We wait. Mac gets wrapped up in a TV sitcom. I reminisce about the day so far.

At breakfast I'd asked Mac what we should do to celebrate your birthday. "Have cake—chocolate cake," he responded without hesitation. "Then we should go for a walk. Mom is in the wind. I want to talk to her."

I make arrangements to be excused from the conference so Mac and I can be alone for lunch. At lunch, Mac and I recount memories of birthdays with you. The day always started with breakfast in bed. Julia and I would make a "fancy" main course— Belgian waffles or those thick cinnamon sugarcoated pancakes that Julia loved. Mac would squeeze orange juice. I'd make coffee from freshly ground beans and search for our special birthday plates—pottery hand painted by Julia at a clay camp she attended one sum-

mer. Cards and presents would be placed in the side
of the serving tray. A bud vase with a fresh-cut rose
would be carried separately so that it would not tip
over on the walk upstairs. We'd form a procession
and would begin singing "Happy Birthday" just as
we approached the hall leading to our bedroom.

You'd feign total surprise. "I can't believe it,"
you'd exclaim. "You did all this for me? Everything
looks so beautiful! It smells go good! You must have
been up for hours. You people are so terrific! I'm so
lucky!"

Then you would playfully negotiate with Mac and
Julia about whether you should eat the food while
it was hot or open the presents first. Regardless of
what they would say, you would always come to the
conclusion that the presents took priority over hot
food. Mac would want his card and present opened
first. Julia would reluctantly accede. You would fawn
over the presents, and when you were done opening them and eating half of the food—"I'm just too
exited to eat any more, but it's *so* good; I'm going to
save it and finish it later," you would state, categori-
cally, "This is *the best* birthday I've ever had in my
whole life."

When Julia got older, she would challenge you.
"That's what you said last year, Mom. You said last
year that it was *the best* birthday of your life. What
makes this one better than last year? Last year I gave

you that red scarf I knitted myself. This year I just got you a cheap store-bought book. How can this year be better than last? You're just saying that!"

"I love the scarf you made for me. I wear it every day in the winter. It's my favorite! But this year, what I really needed was that book. It's just what I've been wanting to read. And look at that rose," you would reply. "It's just magnificent. The color is so deep. How could God make anything more perfect than that?"

For Mac, hyperbole wasn't an issue. He seems to understand intuitively that the present moment is always "the best ever"—always better than *anything* historical. So Mac would get bored with the debate, give you a hug, and head off to listen to music—"the best ever" music, in his mind.

"It doesn't seem right to be talking about Mom's birthdays as if Mom isn't here," Mac breaks in as I'm reminiscing about our ongoing debate about exaggeration. And the birthday cake has arrived—without candles. I ask the waitress if the restaurant has candles. "We don't normally have candles here," she replies. "But a couple ordered some for a party today, and they just cancelled their reservation. I can't see why you couldn't have one."

We sing "Happy Birthday." Mac blows out the candle and says, "Let's go for a walk."

"Would you like to take these flowers with you?" our waitress asks as we depart. "They're yours. The same couple with the candles ordered a dozen roses. They'll just dry up if you don't take them. And 'Happy Birthday,' by the way."

Mac and I take the roses and drive to a park. We have the park to ourselves: the skiers are long gone; it's too early for the "leafers" who will inundate Colorado next month. A small path winds through the grove of aspen trees. We follow it to a small creek that meanders through the park. We stop. We listen to the sound of water in the creek as it embraces rocks and then lets them go. At the waterfall, droplets of water rise momentarily from the creek and then rejoin the flow of the stream at the pool below.

"Do droplets of water experience themselves as 'separate' when they leave the stream over the waterfall?" I wonder half aloud. "Is the stream an accumulation of millions of droplets of water come together—like sand forming a beach? Or is the droplet part of an organic whole that becomes separated in the waterfall as part of a natural cycle—like leaves from a tree?" There's so little I understand, Nancy.

"How about we float the roses down the creek?" I ask Mac. "You remember when we floated the flowers down Spring Lake Creek?" Mac nods, and one at a time each of us places a flower in the stream. They form a procession as they float lazily down the creek. One gets caught in an eddy and rotates dizzyingly until, by happenstance, it is freed by a twig entering the eddy.

After all of the roses have disappeared over the small waterfall, we walk back to our car. We are greeted by a sudden gust of wind. Mac breathes in the air. "Mom says that this was her best birthday, the *best ever*," announces Mac.

My reminiscing is interrupted by the ring of the telephone. It's Julia. "Are you OK?" I ask. "It's hours past when you were going to call."

"I'm fine, Dad. I just didn't get back to the *finca* until a couple of minutes ago. What happened is that I ran into this guy from Britain who has been hiking Peru for a month. We got to chatting. He started to tell me about this terrific creek with a waterfall that runs into the Urubamba River. It's not on any of the maps. You can get to it only by hiking up the face of a cliff after biking five miles down a tiny dirt path.

"Well, it's Mom's birthday and all. I've got this association of Mom with creeks, what with her always walking to Spring Lake Creek and then our having scattered ashes there last year. So I asked him for directions, and before I knew it, we had ended up renting some bicycles. At first I was concerned that I'd have to talk to him and keep him company—I just wanted to be by myself and with my thoughts about Mom. But he was completely quiet. It turned out perfect. I could never have found the place on my

own. When we got back, he said 'hasta luego,' and
disappeared.

"When we got to the creek, I just sat mesmerized
by the rushing water. Have you ever noticed how
water droplets separate and then they come back together? It's as if separateness is just an illusion.

"I felt really connected to Mom. I sat there for a
long time. And after sitting for what must have been
close to an hour, I felt moved to pick some wild flowers and toss them into the stream. I realize that this
is something that I can always do on Mom's birthday
wherever I happen to be—find a body of moving
water and cast a flower in it. I think I'll make a ritual
of it. What did you and Mac do?"

I related our experience at the restaurant and
our ending up floating a dozen roses over a waterfall.
"Was the cake chocolate?" asked Julia. "Of course," I
replied. "It is Mom's birthday. It couldn't have been
anything else."

"I thought I needed to do something with chocolate too," said Julia. "But of course getting a cake
would have been kind of hard—and a total waste
since I still refuse to eat chocolate. So I bought a
Peruvian candy bar at a small *tienda*, but they had
no candles. Then I noticed a family sitting around a
table eating in the back of the *tienda* under candle-
light and asked if they would sell me a candle. 'Just
one candle?' the father asked and gave it to me as a

regalito. I stuck the candle in the candy bar and sang 'Happy Birthday' to Mom sitting by myself at a little outdoor table in front of the *tienda*. You'll be proud of me, Dad. I relaxed my standards and even took a small bite of the chocolate candy bar in Mom's honor.

"This isn't the first birthday since Mom died. I thought it would be easier. But it isn't. I have so many things to tell her. It's like things aren't complete until I've recounted them to her. It all sits in this gigantic suspense file waiting to be retold. I'm not sure there's enough room in the file to hold it all. I love talking to you, Dad. And I feel like I can get a lot off my chest. But it just isn't the same. I feel like even after I've told you about what has happened in my life, it still won't be complete until I've told Mom about it. Does that make any sense to you?"

"I always tell Mom what happens in *my* life," interrupts Mac. "Mom promised me she'd always be in my heart. Do you want me to tell her about your stuff too, Julia? I know Mom is here. And she says that she loves you."

"I'm not sure I can have the same kind of conversations with Mom that you do, Mac," Julia responds. "It doesn't work for me to pretend that she is here when I know she isn't. I miss her so!"

Julia and I sob on the phone. I tell her I'm sorry you died, Nancy. But I don't tell her I know how it feels. We sit holding our phones in silence. I've learned that *I* don't know how *anything* feels for someone else. But as we sit in silence, I'm drawn to reflect again on the droplets of water that make up the creek. My pain is like one of those droplets of water—momentarily experienced by me as separate from the rest of the pain in the world. I mistakenly imagine that it originates from me in relationship to you, rather than originating from the stream of which pain itself is a part.

I finally break the silence. "You know I sometimes experience myself as separate from the rest of the water—like one of those droplets going over the waterfall. But my separateness, Mom's separateness, your separateness—they are all illusions when looked at from a larger perspective. When you look at the waterfall from a distance, you don't see droplets of water separated from their source; you see one integrated whole—a majestic waterfall. Does this make any sense to you?"

"Sort of," Julia responds. "I guess it's all about fear. If the droplet thinks that it will never rejoin the main body of water, it's going to be scared. I think my fear is not so much about being motherless as the implications—what if there is nothing beyond the material world? What if the physical realm really is all that there is? That's what scares me the most, and Mom's not being around brings it all into question."

"Did Mom ever say anything to you when she

was alive about how to get in touch with the non-material realm?" I asked, rhetorically.

"She'd just tell me to listen, to listen to the quiet voice within—to pray without asking for something specific. She'd tell me that I'd experience the answers in my body and my heart, not my mind. She'd tell me that Albert Einstein said that the most basic question is whether or not the universe is a friendly place. She'd say that when you're open to seeing the universe as a friendly place, you start letting yourself take in things—even little things—as miracles."

"That guy showing up and guiding you to the creek leading into the Urubamba. The waitress having candles and roses for Mac and me. Our 'just happening' to go to a park that 'just happened' to have a creek with a tiny waterfall. I'm not sure they rise to the level of miracles. But they sure made our day unfold differently than if they hadn't happened," I observe.

"You're right, Dad. Did I tell you that the guy that showed me the way just disappeared after we got back? It's like he was an angel. He was there just to guide me, and when his mission was done, he was nowhere to be seen. The experience I had at the creek was incredible. It was so indescribably beautiful. I felt so connected to Mom. I can't imagine the day without it. And then there was that family at the *tienda* that happened to have candles. It would never have occurred to me to search for a store that had candles just to put one on a chocolate bar. This whole trip in Peru has been like that—things just seem to come up when I need them. Some days I feel like I've just been on some magical carpet."

"What will you do tomorrow?" I ask.

"Well, we're going to hike the Inca Trail to Machu Picchu. I had this tour arranged through the university. But there weren't enough people with advanced hiking experience. So they had to cancel it at the last minute. I was really disappointed that I wouldn't be able to go. At dinner, I was talking to my friend Cecilia about rigorous hiking, and a professor I didn't even know—from the archaeology department—stopped and said that he had overheard our conversation. He said he was doing research on the spiritual lives of the Incas, and one of his research assistants had become ill. He asked if I'd be interested in coming along. So I'm getting to not only hike the Inca Trail, but I'll have access to some of the ancient sacred sites that are not open to the public. They're supposed to be magnificent. It's like the inner sanctum for the entire civilization. It's the kind of place Mom would have really liked."

Julia paused.

"Maybe I'll try talking to Mom about it while I'm there," Julia added.

with all my love,

Dear
Nancy,

Paz
a todos los que vienen aqui
les invitamos a unirse al
Silencio
de este lugar para escuchar a
Dios.

Perhaps the author of the sign just meant to say "quiet." Perhaps a circle with the word "noise" and a slanted line through it would have conveyed the essence of the message.

But here, in Santiago, Chile, atop San Cristobal, where Mac and I visit Julia during her semester abroad, we read much more:

Peace
to all who come here
we invite you to unite with the
Silence

of this place in order to listen to
God.

Moved by the lyrical rhythm of the words, as well as
the profundity of the message, I translate a second time
for Mac. He is unimpressed. "It's just the same as listening to Mom," he says. "Whether it is God or Mom,
all you have to do is be silent and listen. Then you can
hear. You can hear her in your ear, and you can hear
her in your heart. She's there."

For Julia, Mac, and me, this year has been a year of
intentional listening. All too often, the sounds are too
subtle for Julia and me to discern. It is Mac who seems
to be better attuned. But Julia and I know that Mac is
right: it is in silence that we open the channel for hearing. It is in silence that we connect to the ineffable.

For Julia, observing silence has meant not giving
anyone, not even her dad, her mailing address in
Santiago. It has meant journaling. Observing silence
has meant taking trips by herself throughout Chile
in solitude—bicycling in the Atacama desert to the
north, walking among penguins in Punta Arenas to
the south, and sunning on Easter Island to the west.

For me, observing silence has meant sailing with
Julia in the British Virgin Islands without racing or
competing. It has meant listening to stories from folks
at the Drop-In Center without working on solving

what I used to identify as their "problems." It has meant meditating during a week-long silent retreat with Marie. It has meant more walks in the woods at our wilderness retreat and less trail blazing. Observing silence has meant heeding the call to take the time to write these letters to you.

For Mac, observing silence has meant living almost every moment present to divine revelation. Wherever he is—at the grocery store "bagging," achieving a black belt in karate, being "independent" by traveling to Colorado with his buddies to ski without me, or attending the National Down Syndrome Congress convention in Phoenix—Mac finds moments to, as he says, "feel" you in the breeze and "listen" to your voice in his heart. Mac continues to be our teacher and our guide.

Peace.

Silence.

God.

Since your death, all three have become a more meaningful presence in our lives. Thank you, Nancy, for this legacy you have left us.

with all my love,

Dear
Nancy,

    I'm going through another death in my
life. Well, it's not really a death in *my* life. It's in our
friend Paul's. And in truth, it's not a death—in the
traditional sense. It's Paul and Sue's marriage that's
dying.

    On the surface, not much has changed. They're
still separated. They're still "moving forward" with
the legal process. They still feign loving attention to
each other, as best they can, in front of the kids. But
they've stopped seeing a marriage counselor. Paul has
given up hope of reconciliation.

    Paul misses you. He misses your empathetic listen-
ing. He misses the historical perspective you brought
to listening, having been a close friend to both him
and Sue during their entire twenty-year roller-coaster
marriage. He misses confiding in someone who was
as understanding to Sue's point of view as his own.

    When I talk to Paul, I problem solve—a part of
the male blueprint, I suspect. So when Paul relates
instances of Sue's continuing sexual indiscretions,

I respond with outrage. When I see Sue's alcohol-induced behavior confuse their children, I offer unsolicited advice to Paul about the psychological effect on their kids.

You rarely offered solutions. You just listened. You listened to Paul. You listened to Sue. Though each knew that the other was also confiding in you, both of them felt safe that you wouldn't take sides. Paul doesn't feel the same safety with me. Yet he feels the need to open his heart to someone with a personal history that goes back before he even met Sue. I'm his confidant by process of elimination.

Last Friday, Paul's children were at Sue's, and I'd invited Paul over for dinner. As soon as Paul arrived, I could tell he had something heavy weighing on his heart. There was light conversation during dinner. After dinner, we sat by the fireplace. Paul sat in silence while I tended to the fire. We'd run out of superficial topics.

Paul finally broke the silence. "This may sound a bit disrespectful to you," he announced.

As you know, Nancy, Paul is one of the gentlest human beings I've ever known. I've never heard him swear. I've never heard him raise his voice. I couldn't imagine what Paul could say that would be disrespectful to me. I stopped rearranging logs to give him my full attention.

"I hope you won't take what I'm going to say in

the wrong way. But at times I'm envious that your marriage ended in death. I think death may be easier than divorce."

Paul must have noticed my furrowed forehead. "I don't mean to say the loss of Nancy has been easy for you," he quickly added. "Nancy's death has been difficult for me: I feel like I've lost a friend, a sister, and a confidant, all wrapped in one. I can only imagine how hard it must be for you."

I nodded.

"But this is the point I wanted to make: you've gone through the death of a person you love. I'm going through the death of the love of a person. The death of love may be even harder than the death of a loved one."

Paul paused. He had slumped down in the couch. "I know I feel completely devastated. My heart is broken. And I'm not sure I'm going to ever recover."

Paul and I have been friends since grade school. He was the best man at our wedding. I love Paul like the brother I never had. But I must admit, Nancy, I was hurt by what Paul said. I couldn't believe he was comparing his divorce to your death.

"I'm not sure I get it," I said to Paul. "Seems to me like the death of love and the death of a *loved one* are pretty hard comparisons to make. What do you mean?"

"Well, I've been observing how your love for

Nancy continues despite her death," Paul replied. "I see the way you honor her. You speak lovingly of her presence even now, more than a year after she died. You still wear Nancy's wedding ring. I see the way Mac communicates with Nancy almost as if he were channeling her. Nancy's physical body has died. But your relationship is alive. For me, it's just the opposite. Sue is alive. But our relationship is dead. It hurts so much."

"It doesn't look to *me* like your love has died." I couldn't help offering advice. "Look at the facts. You've been separated for four years now, and you still can't finalize the divorce—all because you feel so committed to Sue. She's been running around with other men for a decade. Most men would have said, 'Enough of this crap,' long ago."

"That's water under the bridge." Paul refused to get into a debate with me. "I've forgiven her. It's part and parcel of the disease. Alcoholism wrecks families. I've learned that I am powerless over the disease. But I'm not powerless over my response. I vowed to stand by Sue 'in sickness and in health.' How can I not stand by her now, when she's sick?"

I wished you were at my side, Nancy. You'd have known what to say to Paul. I didn't. I sat in a trance-like state, staring through Paul and nodding my head. I tried to reconstruct in my mind what you had said to other friends when their marriages fell apart. I

remembered Fred leaving your best friend Marilyn
just three weeks after the adoption of their first
child. "How could Fred be such a jerk?" I recall asking you rhetorically. "Running off at a time like this!
Does the man have no shame?"

But you counseled forgiveness. "The energy
you put out is what comes back to you," you said to
Marilyn. "Imagine how difficult it must be for him
to live with what he's done. Think how blessed you
are in not having to be in his shoes."

"Paul," I eventually responded. "You've done
everything a human being can possibly do. You've
been through counseling with Sue. You've tried to
get her into treatment. You've cried, blamed, begged,
threatened, pleaded, bargained. But Sue is too high
functioning! It's easy for her to be in denial about
her addiction. Don't they say in AA that an alcoholic
has to 'hit bottom' before she can start the path to
recovery? Perhaps, by holding on, you're holding Sue
back from hitting bottom."

"I'm not holding on. *I'm* the one who moved out
of the house. *I'm* the 'petitioner' on the legal papers
to dissolve the marriage. And now I feel *I'm* the one
who bears the responsibility for the death of our
marriage."

"What you're going through sounds to me like
grieving," I replied. I suggested he was grieving the
loss of a dream—the dream of a perfect marriage.

And that he was blaming himself for the death of the dream.

"Self-blame can be completely irrational," I said. "There is a woman in my grief group who blames herself for her husband's death even though he died in a fluke car accident, hit by a drunk driver. She's convinced that if she'd made breakfast for him that day, he'd have left for work a couple of minutes later and wouldn't have been killed. Aren't you falling into the same trap?" I asked Paul. "It seems to me that if anyone is to be blamed for what's happened to your marriage, it's Sue, or it's booze."

"There's something to what you say." Paul sat up straighter. "Guilt was drummed into me early. I was an altar boy, you know. I remember once feeling guilty because a friend of mine was punished for throwing water balloons at some nuns. I wasn't even there."

A smile was starting to break through Paul's granite countenance. He asked if I wanted to hear the story. I nodded.

"I'd joked with one of the other altar boys about how funny it would be to toss a water balloon in the midst of the nuns in the convent. They never smiled. They never appeared excited. They were so officious. I wanted to see if we could crack their serious shell.

"But I never considered getting real balloons and filling them with real water—and I never dreamed that my friend would do it alone. One day, without telling me, my friend lobbed balloons filled with yellow dyed water at the nuns walking together to morning mass. I cried with laughter when he told how the nuns crashed into each other to avoid the exploding balloons. But I immediately felt guilty that I'd laughed. I actually went to confession—I guess to confess the sin of just *wishing* I'd been there to see the havoc."

"So what do you think you might be feeling guilty about with Sue? Is your lawyer taking a tough stance on custody?"

"No. The stipulation is pretty much worked out. Sue's the mother of my children—and always will be. She needs to spend time with them. But with Sue's drinking getting worse and worse, joint custody just isn't the right thing. Sue's lawyer advised her not to push it, as I was willing to assure that they'd spend lots of time together.

"I think I've inadvertently made things worse by being helpful. The other day she had a problem with her car insurance. I called the agent and took care of it for her. I think she felt my thoughtful attention to such details in her life is the kind of thing a loving husband would do, not the 'petitioner' in a divorce proceeding."

I wanted to be helpful to Paul. Yet I knew I didn't have the words that would mitigate his self-doubt. I

groped in my memory for what you might say, knowing all the time that you probably wouldn't say anything. Just actively listening would make it possible
for Paul to go within to find his own answers. At
most, you'd put your hand on Paul's shoulder. Why
couldn't I bring myself to make that simple gesture?

So rather than doing what you would have done,
I counseled that Paul didn't have to stop being loving toward Sue just because their marriage hasn't
worked out. That he will always have a relationship
with Sue. And I suggested that having a relationship
with her—even a loving relationship—doesn't mean
that he needs to stay married to her.

Paul sat looking at the flames of the fire.

"You've told me that since your separation, you've
loved Sue as a sister, not a wife," I continued. "Is
that the kind of marriage relationship you want? To
be married to your sister?"

"Everything you say is true," sighed Paul. "I think
you just don't understand the depth of the conflict
I feel. No matter what I do, I feel like I'll end up
in hell. If I go forward with my marriage, I'll be
damned by a relationship that is dysfunctional and
damaging to Sue, to me, and to the children. If I pro-
ceed with the divorce, I'll be damned by breaching
my marital vows in failing to stand by my wife in her
illness. I feel like I'm living out some Greek myth in
which there's no way to avoid a fate of damnation."

We sat in silence.

"I just want to have things the way they were," Paul moaned. "I want to love Sue like I did when we were first married. I want her to love me back. I so miss Nancy. She would have understood how difficult this is. I keep wondering what she would have said."

The fire had started to die out. I put on another log. The dry wood caught immediately and burst into flames along its entire length. I stood for a moment, mesmerized by the oranges, reds, and purples of the flame. When I sat down, it was on the couch beside Paul, not the armchair I'd been sitting in before.

"I think I'm having such a hard time coming up with what Nancy would have said to me because I'm not sure she would have said anything to me," Paul said after the flames of the fire were burning bright once again. "She would just listen to me with complete attentiveness. It always seemed like there wasn't another thing in the world that mattered to her when she was listening to me. I never felt like her mind was trying to come up with a response to what I was saying. I didn't feel like she was taking sides. She was just there, accepting what was happening without judgment or analysis. That made it possible to hear myself. It was like I had all of the answers I needed, but it was too dark to see. Nancy helped turn on the light for me to see the answer that was inside me all along."

"Maybe we've been doing too much talking and not enough listening to the voices within," I said. "We could both use a breath of fresh air." I suggested that we go for a walk around Lake Harriet. "The cold air will do us good."

Nancy, this winter each snowfall has melted within days. Mac's snow pants and boots are still upstairs in winter storage. And with temperatures rarely below freezing, much of January has felt almost balmy. But last Friday a strong wind was blowing out of the north. Temperatures had dropped into the low teens.

I loaned Paul your black woolen scarf. We wore stocking caps that I retrieved from the winter storage shelf.

As Paul and I felt the icy wind across the frozen lake, I remembered that even temperatures well below zero would not deter you from your daily walk around Lake Harriet. "The really cold days are the most empowering for the soul," I remember you saying to me. "Everyone's bundled so. People hunch over and look down just to keep their faces out of the wind. The weather forces you to go completely within."

Paul and I walked in silence. I tried to keep from thinking about Paul and his divorce, about you and your absence from my life, about the listener that you were for Paul, about the listener you were for me, about losses—the loss of love, the loss of life. I pretended it was one of those below zero days with the wind blowing like razor blades across the lake, one of those days that you said forced you completely within. Deep within. Not into my head. Not into my heart. Completely within, to my soul.

I listened. I listened to the beat of my pulse against the elastic band of my stocking cap. I felt the difference in temperature between the skin on my exposed cheeks and on my covered ears. The cold wind buffeted my winter parka. I felt a heaviness cover my sternum, the spot my grief group facilitator contends is the "grief point." The heaviness there felt like a medieval breastplate. It was made of thick iron, held to my chest with large leather straps pulled over my shoulders, and crisscrossed on my back. It spoke to me, saying that its purpose was to protect my heart from being broken.

I allowed myself to experience the metallic texture of the breastplate against my skin. I felt the shield it created against letting in Paul's pain. The armor slowly began to dissolve. My heart was exposed. I felt tears deep inside my heart that did not wet my eyes. As those deep tears were cried, the heaviness of the breastplate abated.

By the time Paul and I arrived back at our home, the fire had almost died out. Coals still glowed below the grate.

"Should I throw on another log?"

"Sure," I responded. We pulled the chairs up right next to the fire. The log started to smolder and finally caught flame. We warmed our hands, comforted by the knowledge that as long as even a few embers are still glowing, a fire will come right back to life again.

My body began to thaw. "As we walked the lake, Paul, I think I opened a bit more to the grief you're feeling at the loss of your marriage. I suppose divorce can be a slow painful death. I'm sorry."

"Thanks. I suppose death isn't easy whether it's slow or fast."

"I wonder, though, what it is, Paul, that's really taking such a long time to die."

"What do you mean?" Paul raised his voice slightly. "You know what's dying. My marriage is dying."

"But something else is dying too, I suspect." I told Paul that I realized that what might be dying for him is the same thing that I've realized has been dying for me since you died: illusion of control. The illusion that we have some power over what happens in our lives. The illusion that we can influence the course of how things will turn out. The illusion that our judgments and analyses make a difference.

I sat next to Paul looking into the flames of the fire, which were now devouring the logs in bright oranges, greens, and blues. One of the logs hissed as steam escaped. In just moments, the few remaining embers had burst into a wild blaze. My judgments, and the illusion that I could control outcomes, were like the fire. For a moment, I would listen to Paul the way you did, attentively and openly. My judgments would come close to dying. But then, they would easily reignite. I would be back to analyzing and problem solving. Even the tiniest ember left glowing was sufficient to reignite the illusion of control that then burst back into bright flame.

That's why you walked the lake, wasn't it, Nancy? Especially on those subzero days—the days when you said everyone was forced to turn within. It was to enter the void, leaving the illusion of control out in the biting cold. For you, Nancy, that illusion was weak and dying long before your diagnosis of cancer. For a moment, as I felt the breastplate of judging armor dissolve the other night, my illusion of control momentarily felt a deathblow. But I realize that Paul and I have a lot more dying to do before we are ready to fully accept life.

with all my love,

Dear
Nancy,

> *Andy and Marie.*
> *Sitting in a tree.*
> *K-I-S-S-I-N-G.*
> *First comes love.*
> *Then comes marriage.*
> *Then comes Mac in a baby carriage.*

Mac sang in a high-pitched voice, holding the rhyming syllables until he was almost out of breath. Hand gestures went along with the ditty: Head tilted to one side. Hands cradled to make a pillow for his cheek. Lips puckered. His eyes twinkled. He was back in grade school during recess. Marie and I were love-birds, but we were not kissing. He was egging us on.

Then, suddenly, he became serious. His smile faded, and the mocking gestures disappeared. He sat down. His back became straight. He leaned forward. "What would your wife say if she saw you kissing Marie?" Mac's voice no longer had a singsong lilt.

Not, "what would *Mom* say." Not, "what would

Nancy say." But, instead, "what would *your wife* say?" We were about to have a meaningful conversation.

How was I to respond to this question from a boy who in his entire life had seen me kiss only one woman—you? That his was a hypothetical question—I'd not actually kissed Marie—made it no easier. Mac accurately sensed love in the air. Fidelity had been brought into question.

Mac adores Marie. He calls her his "special friend" and invites her over (without consulting me) to just "hang out." They go on walks by themselves, and though he is careful to remind her that she is *a* mother, not *his* mother, he confides in her like he felt he could with you, not me. Marie listens without problem solving. When your absence overcomes him, he allows himself to collapse into her lap. I suspect Mac hopes we will kiss. I suspect he hopes we will marry. At the same time, he is afraid. Is he being a traitor to his mother? His egging us on brings into question his own fidelity, not just mine.

I dreaded responding to Mac's question. Any reasoned response seemed too philosophical and complicated. I recall the conversations you and I had about remarrying if one of us should die. Would Mac make sense of my recounting them? Could he understand that we'd had conversations about death since we were his age? Would he understand that our sense of the love we experienced was not *our love* but a participation in something larger than us? Could I tell Mac that when love is larger than either of us, it doesn't depend upon us? Nancy, I feel lost without you. The world of complex emotions is the world *you* handled. I take clients to lunch and talk about capital markets. I feel comfortable speaking intelligibly about merger candidates, not marriage candidates.

I think I do know the answer to Mac's question of what you, Nancy, would have said about my kissing Marie. You would have said, "Kiss her harder. Kiss her longer." You would have said, "Don't wait for the 'appropriate' time. Don't heed tribal rules." You would have reminded me that love is a divine gift. You would have told me that love doesn't come from me, it comes from a higher power. "It's sacred," I can hear you saying. "Don't squander it."

You might have even talked about how you scanned the country to find someone who could love Mac, Julia, and me with your same gentle acceptance. You might even have mentioned how easy it would have been for me, had I been left to my own devices, to end up with a playmate instead of a mature mother of four grown children. It wasn't easy, was it, for you to arrange my meeting Marie—to have my path cross with someone who doesn't ski, go to the symphony, read Kant, Hegel, or Sartre. Someone who, instead, tends to hearts.

"Don't screw it up," you would have said. "Love her. Don't *talk* about loving her."

"You learned a lot about loving in the last months of my life," you would have reminded me. "Love her the way you loved *me* those months. Love her the way I loved *you* since third grade."

You'd remind me of the biblical parable about the master who entrusts his goods to his three servants for safekeeping, rewarding the two who used and multiplied what they'd been given for safekeeping, and castigating the servant who buried the riches to keep them safe. You'd caution me that there are risks attendant to burying our gifts: they may be taken away, just like they were from the third servant. What is given us is meant to be enjoyed and celebrated. Then, and only then, does it multiply. So it is with love. So it is with kisses.

What was I to say to Mac? Certainly not a sermonette based on a biblical parable. So I ducked the question and sought to divert attention from me to Mac. After a long silence, I finally replied.

"What do *you* think my wife would say, Mac?"

"I think Mom would kiss you with Marie's lips," he replied. Then, without hesitation, he went on. "What's for dinner, Dad?"

with all my love,

Dear
Nancy,

Today the dining room is decorated with streamers—the same green, red, yellow, and blue ones that you always made sure were retrieved for family celebrations from the party chest in the attic. I've put out bright confetti-patterned napkins for the table. The Chinese accordion lanterns have been hung from the dining room chandelier and from the wall sconces. But the party chest still appears full.

I'd forgotten what a storehouse of party games, candles, paper plates, and napkins we've accumulated over the years. The chest contains celebratory banners for all imaginable occasions—birthdays, graduations, homecomings. I even ran across a large banner in big bold letters reading "Congratulations on Your Retirement." Was that banner ever used, Nancy? When?

After looking through the banners a second and third time, I'm still unable to locate the silvery Mylar Happy Birthday banner. I catch myself wondering if

I've misplaced it. Without you here, it seems like so many things can't be found.

Then I vaguely remember that the banner was ripped when I was taking it down after a birthday party. Would that have been Mac's birthday last March? It couldn't have been mine, I reason. My June birthday is less than three weeks before the date of your death. We wouldn't have celebrated a birthday, with the entire extended family here, that close to the day you died, would we?

But then, again, why not? You were vibrant and energetic even then. You wouldn't have cooked, but a party could have otherwise gone on as usual. You so loved celebrations. You so loved giving parties. You might well have insisted on my birthday party being held here.

I'm aware that this is not the first occasion on which I find myself trying to reconstruct what must have happened by linking together the "possibles" and rejecting the "impossibles." I find myself piecing the "possibles" together in a giant jigsaw puzzle in my mind and then saying to myself, "Yes. *That's* what happened." Since you died, I feel I've stopped being able to recall things directly from memory.

A block-lettered sign, handmade by Chad, takes the place of the Mylar banner I've been unable to locate. It is taped behind Mac's seat. I notice that it seems strangely out of place with the rest of the

decorations that have bedecked the dining room so
many times. Though the streamers clash with the
lanterns and the party hats have seemed childish to
me for years, they have a coordinated "correctness"
to them. The new sign is out of place.

As I look more closely, I see that it's not only the
banner that's off. The colors of the streamers and the
accordion lanterns don't seem to have their usual
intensity. The birthday place mats seem to have yel-
lowed. But it's only been a year since they were out
last. It can't be sitting in the attic that's made them
fade. Nancy, it is your energy that is missing.

Mac sits at the head of the table. My mother sits
to his right. At the far end of the table, Dana chats
with Kera, who has flown in from Denver for the
weekend. Chad and Mark are engaged in a heated
discussion about the public school system. I suspect
the debate may well be the same one heard here exactly a year ago. Everyone is talking. No one is listening. Only you, Nancy, could command the attention
of the entire group of assembled relatives.

Mac still eschews cakes—even birthday cakes. I've
had Baskin-Robbins make an immense ice cream
pie for him instead. It's decorated with *Star Trek*
characters—Seven of Nine and Captain Janeway,
who've become Mac's new passion. The candles are
lit. Julia and I walk ceremoniously into the dining
room singing "Happy Birthday."

Singing provides a momentary unification of focus. But just as soon as the last stanza has been sung, the countless conversations are resumed in mid-sentence. Without you here, the group is leaderless.

Then, abruptly, Mac rises from his chair and lifts both arms above his head. "Wait," he says. "I w-w-want to do something."

"Do you want to open presents, Mac?" suggests Dana.

"Yes. But not yet. First, I want everyone to do one thing as a g-group."

A hush falls on the room. All eyes are riveted on Mac. I can sense that for some, not knowing what will come next is uncomfortable. However, I recognize that everyone present has experienced this same discomfort before. Right here. In this room.

Like Mac today, you'd take charge of the assembled relatives. You'd guide them to share their concerns and feelings with the entire group. The heated discussions would stop. Kera and Mark would listen. We'd learn new things about each other. Relationships would sometimes be healed. Yet, at the next family gathering, Mark or Fran would apprehensively joke about leaving before your "touchy-feely" séances.

"Look into the flame," Mac commands pointing at the candle in the center of the table. "Look into the flame and then close your eyes."

Mac stands in silence. Then, after checking to make sure that everyone's eyes are still closed, Mac continues in an authoritative voice. "My mom is here." Mac pauses between sentences. They are delivered as commandments. "She wipes away my tears. She makes me happy.

"She is proud of me for I am now a teenage m-m-man with responsibilities. She is happy you are here with me." The slight crackling sound of the flame licking fresh wax fills the room.

"Mom's spirit is in this room and in each of you. Before I open presents, I need a hug from everyone. When you hug me, my mom hugs me."

Then, Mac's voice changes, and his tempo modulates from largo to allegro. "So. How about hugs?"

The family lines up to give Mac hugs. Though he has said that your spirit is in *them*, it is Mac who hugs each family member with the intensity of your energy. A soft serenity emanates as they leave the line. Voices are lowered. The debates and animated conversations do not recommence. Our dining room has been transformed into a sacred space.

"What was that all about?" asks Dana as we load the dishwasher. "I can't believe Mac's presence. It's not often that someone can get the attention of the entire family for more than a second or two. And even then, someone usually cracks a joke. Mac's really quite charismatic. That bit with the candle was something else! It was like a séance or something. Where did Mac get that?"

"You're not asking if it was orchestrated, are you? You know that I'd never have the ability to stage-manage something that artfully."

"That's what's so spooky. It really felt like Nancy was there in the room and that Mac was somehow channeling her. Mac doesn't usually talk in that tone of voice. It almost felt like it wasn't Mac's phonetics being formed by his own lips—like Mac's lips were being moved by some other force."

My mother has already started wiping the counters. She wants to know where to put the pans. "The housekeeper is coming tomorrow," I lie. "She'll finish up here, Mom. You don't need to do this. Let's relax in the study for a minute and have a cup of coffee."

My mother insists she doesn't want a cup of coffee. She says she doesn't want the cleaning lady to clean. If there's cleaning to be done, she's going to do it. Ninety-one years of age are not going to deter her. I'm not going to deter her. "I'll just tidy up a couple of things here. You go tend to your guests now," she says.

"They're not guests," I respond. "They're family."

"Family are the most important guests," my mother declares resolutely. "Experience them the way that Mac experiences Nancy. Then they will be as alive to you as Nancy is to him." My mother is done wiping the counters.

"Most people take Nancy for granted because her body is not here. You take your guests for granted because they're family. Mac sees beyond the self-evident. You need to see more deeply. You're entertaining royalty, my son. Your family are what *you* see in them—nothing more, nothing less. Who is in your living room at this moment depends entirely on the limitations of your *eyesight*, not on the costumes being worn."

I ask my mother if she is suggesting that Mac's eyesight somehow transcends the laws of physics.

"I'm getting too old to intellectualize," my mother replies. "I don't know physics. Physics is just another vocabulary. Vocabulary intimidates those who don't know the vocabulary. And it gives a false sense of security to those who do know it. The vocabulary we know—English, psychology, Western mythology—this vocabulary gives *us* a false sense of security."

We stand, my mother leaning against the counter. I against the refrigerator. Animated debates can be heard emanating from the living room.

"Vocabulary doesn't provide answers. It's an abstraction that represents something else. The word 'eat' is not eating. The word 'love' is not loving.

You eat by putting food in your mouth. You love by embracing another. Words just make you an expert. They don't nourish. In fact, they have the opposite effect—they distance you from experiencing the mysterious. It is experiencing the mysterious that nourishes us.

"Mac's not encumbered by being an expert. His vocabulary in English, psychology, and Western mythology is not as developed as ours. He's blessed. He's able to experience the unknown and enter into the mystery because he doesn't make the same assumptions we've been taught by our culture. Son, go bow to your royalty."

I put down the dishcloth. I look into my mother's eyes and bow to her with my hands at my chest like Lapsam did over and over. I catch a gleam in her eye. It is *your* twinkle, Nancy. I stand transfixed for a moment, kiss my mother gently on the forehead, and walk with her under my arm into the living room to "pay homage" to my royalty. We walk through the dining room. The streamers glisten. The Chinese lanterns burst with orange and green.

with all my love,

Dear
Nancy,

It's been almost three years since you died.
I notice that an entire day may now pass without my
being consciously aware of the wound of your death.
But then, invariably, I brush up against something:
a sunset that reminds me of a red sky we watched together at our wilderness retreat, a casual reference by
a friend to the "Drop-In" center for the mentally ill
that you founded, the lingering scent of Chanel No.
5 as a woman hurries from the powder room back to
her seat for the start of the second act at the Guthrie
Theater. It's then that I realize that the wound of
your death is still open—and that it easily bleeds.

It doesn't take colliding head on with something major—like your birthday or our wedding
anniversary—to rip off the scab. Instead, things
that I don't consciously associate with you seem capable of reopening this wound that is now already
30 months old.

One of my earliest childhood memories is of the
deep gash I got on my leg while playing Capture

the Flag with the neighborhood "gang"—including you—when we were in fourth grade. Playing in Kenwood Park after dark had been forbidden by both your parents and mine. Yet, we pretended we'd gone next door to play and, instead, sneaked off to the park. When I came home with a ripped pants leg soaked with blood, I was sure we'd been found out.

I remember being more concerned that I'd be barred from ever going out again than I was about the cut on my calf. But my mother asked me no questions. She fastidiously tended to the wound and let me suffer with the knowledge that my rule breaking had been punished with a cut that would leave a permanent scar. "That's a nasty cut," I recall her saying. "It'll need some air. But, for now, it's important to hold the skin together so that it'll close up fast. Keep the bandage on. If the tape comes loose, come tell me and have it retaped right away so the wound won't reopen."

Forty years later, your cancer taught us just the opposite, didn't it, Nancy? Having wounds close up quickly is not necessarily a sign of healing. In fact, it can even be dangerous.

After your last abdominal surgery, the incision didn't completely close. I can still visualize the six-inch gash with its twenty-five or thirty stitches as clearly as when I first saw it in the surgical recovery room. For the first couple of days, the cut seemed to be growing together. But shortly after we came home, a small opening developed. Days passed. The opening became larger. Your doctor referred to the opening as a "fistula."

The fistula was located just below your navel and was nearly the size of a dime. It festered. For weeks, brown and green pus oozed from the opening. The gauze bandages often became saturated with the lumpy liquid, which would then leak down the side of your stomach and onto the sheets. I recall wiping the ooze from your stomach, changing the bandages, and remaking your bed many times a day. But its rancid odor would linger. We prayed that the fistula would close.

One morning we woke up to find a diaphanous layer of skin covering the opening. There was no green and brown ooze saturating the bandages. There was no leakage that had dripped on the sheets. The fistula had closed. We were elated. I even jokingly suggested a bottle of champagne with lunch. Finally, you were on the mend, we reasoned.

That same afternoon, your home health-care nurse came by to examine the wound. She frowned. "The fistula has grown over from the outside," she said as she began irrigating the wound to reopen it. "Wounds need to be kept open so they can heal from the inside. If a wound closes from the outside first, the body's internal toxins become trapped, and then the body has to create a new fistula to release the poisons.

"Healing takes time. And it must take place from the inside out. You know, surface healing is just what the word means: superficial."

Julia, Mac, and I have learned from your fistula, Nancy. We realize that keeping a wound open is a necessary part of the healing process—and that covering up the wound too soon runs the risk of locking in toxins that then have no avenue of escape. And so, the three of us intentionally irrigate the wound of your death to make sure that it doesn't close up prematurely.

How have we done this? Well, for one, we've not changed any of the pictures on the walls and tables— the photographs of you and of your family, parents, and siblings still occupy their same spaces. They're now imbued with new meaning for Julia, Mac, and me. You might say that they are irrigation for a wound that might otherwise have closed up prematurely.

Your clothes still remain in your closets untouched. Your black cashmere winter car coat hangs in the entryway closet, and I still have to push its hanger aside to reach for my jacket. Your pajamas lie folded in the top drawer of our bedroom bureau though, I must admit, I've thought about trading places with you as I've stooped to reach for my own underwear in the bottom drawer.

Your books and papers occupy their traditional spaces in the butler's pantry and the desk of your study. When I water the plants, I know them to be *your* plants, and I know that I'm performing one of *your* activities. (And I admit that it took nearly two and a half years for me to no longer see watering the plants as a "chore" but, as you did, an opportunity to connect with the plants and nourish them.)

I still wear your wedding ring. I irrigate the wound of your death by consciously affirming that we are still man and wife.

For me, writing these letters irrigates the wound. I find that writing invites me to explore the deepest parts of my soul. Often my eyes water as I put my memories on paper, and I sense that my tears flush out trapped toxins festering inside.

Nancy, I've learned the faces of grief: anger, sadness, regret, relief, and guilt. Each of these feelings is a fistula—an avenue for expressing and releasing grief. Each is also capable of festering and of being covered over from the outside. And though Julia, Mac, and I have expressed much of our grief openly, I realize that, for me, the anger fistula may have closed prematurely.

"Aren't you angry?" my friends keep asking me. "Aren't you just plain outraged that Nancy died at such a young age? Damn it! It just isn't fair."

I ache to say, "Yes. Of course I'm angry." But my

analytical mind quickly takes over. Philosophically, I know that *nothing* is permanent and that judging things as "fair" or "unfair" is useless.

"What's there to be angry *about*?" I debate with myself. Impermanence is a given. Am I angry that the laws of the universe apply also to me?

I affirm, as you did, Nancy, that the universe is a friendly place. I accept, as you did, Nancy, that all things happen in the universe for our good. So should I be angry that God's mind saw things turning out differently than did my mind? Should I be angry that my vision is more limited than God's?

But I also see that our worldview has tended to cover up my anger. I've not railed against God. I've yet to scream out loud, "God, why Nancy? What's *she* done to deserve this? Why *me*? What've *I* done, God, to deserve this? Why? Damn it. Why?" Not yelling out these questions may have kept my anger trapped inside, finding another, indirect fistula for its release.

The week before last, for example, I lost my patience with Mac. We were already ten minutes late for Mac's appointment with the math tutor. He was still in his room methodically deciding which T-shirt to put on. "Can't you *ever* be on time?" I demanded of Mac. "What is wrong with you? You've only got one speed—regardless of the circumstances. Don't you *ever* get tired of being late—or making me wait and wait and wait? Mac, I just won't put up with being your babysitter any longer. You're an adult, for God's sake!"

Nancy, I'm ashamed to have my anger explode all over Mac. Am I supposed to irrigate the fistula? How? Paradoxically, as I become more aware of my impatience with Mac, I notice that my relationship with him deepens. I talk to him about my anger. In reply, he relates episodes of his own anger. The other day, Mac verbalized the feeling of shame he experiences in response to my impatience. I hugged him as I acknowledged that this is just how I felt when my father sat in the car with a furrowed forehead drumming his fingers on the steering wheel while I fumbled to find the sheet music that I'd not practiced since the last piano lesson. I've begun to recognize that there are wounds that are older and deeper than grief. These, too, need irrigation.

So, grief has taught me that awareness opens fistulas. And if I succeed in keeping them open, I've learned that the insights provided promote richer relationships. Nancy, the universe is indeed a friendly place.

with all my love,

from *Gifts of Spirit;* spirituality lecture series,
March 1991

As the old Chinese proverb says: "You cannot prevent the birds of sadness from passing over your head but you can prevent their making nests in your hair."

We need to slow down. We need to act "as if"—as if there's divine order in the universe, as if someone is watching over you, as if your smile will be returned. It's also very important that we acknowledge when we feel synchronicity happen to us—that we bless it. The more we do this, the more it will happen to us.

One of the main obstacles to this spiritual discernment is our self-reliant attitude, which has been so ingrained in us by our culture of individualism. We have to unlearn the human concept of being on our own. We have to actively cultivate a disposition of obedience. I'm sure this word arouses in many of us a negative reaction as we are reminded of people—parents, brothers, spouses, who have ordered us around without kindness. But actually the word obedience comes from the Latin *obaudire*, which means to listen attentively. True obedience implies a relaxed, appreciative heeding of all the happenings in our life as communications of

God. So obedience does not mean searching for amazing accomplishments, stunning feats, or impressive renunciations. It's not a commitment to accomplish as much as possible under adverse conditions. It is a commitment to listen to the mystery speaking in the simple events of everyday life. This is not so easy. Listening is hard. What if we are invited to give up a grudge we have nursed for a lifetime? Obedience may challenge us to accept a responsibility we have ignored—like speaking out against a racist remark, an anti-Semitic joke, not letting our children see violent movies, use vulgar language or not even saying "Oh God" ourselves.

Obedience also happens in community. We realize that the divine mystery speaks not only to us personally but also to our companions on the journey. We listen respectfully to one another in the hope that the mystery may manifest itself to us through one another.

And of course we also pray. We pray that we may align ourselves with this greater order, which runs the universe, that we may be awakened to a more conscious linking to something that is greater.

So our job is to keep asking for truth and to be willing to hear the answer. Problems that come into our lives are door-knockers at the gate of heaven. But the good news is, we don't have to figure it all out. We just bless whatever is happening and ask to discern its gift.

Dear
   Nancy,

Linda unexpectedly died last week, and my friend Nate stopped by to ask me what he could say to best support Linda's husband. He figured that with all of the calls I'd received after your death, I should be able to tell him what to say to George to best console him—and, just as importantly, what not to say.

"George is so swamped with calls," Nate said to me. "I'll probably end up leaving a message on his answering machine—where what I say will be etched in stone."

I knew that the real problem was not the finality of a message on an answering machine. It was that George and Nate hadn't communicated much over the past year. There's unfinished business between them that has nothing to do with Linda's dying. And Nate knew he couldn't very well bring that stuff up now.

"I really don't know what to say," Nate groaned.

"What was the most comforting thing that anyone said to you after Nancy died?"

I didn't have to pause to think about the right answer. It was Greg who'd said just the right thing to me after you died. And Greg kept saying it over and over. It was in part because he said it on my answering machine that it was so comforting. I'll never forget the simplicity of his words as I played back my messages: "Andy, it's Greg calling. I want you to know that I'm here for you. Call me if you want. But don't feel any obligation to return the call. I'll keep calling you."

Greg did. He called me again and again without my having returned any calls. He'd leave exactly the same message—and in a tone that made it clear that he was absolutely sincere that he needed nothing in return from me. Not even a returned phone call to let him know that I appreciated his calls. He told me later that he intentionally called at times that he knew I wasn't by the phone so that he wouldn't burden me with having to talk with him.

"What does your heart tell you to say to George?" I asked Nate. "What would you have said to him if your relationship weren't strained right now?"

"I think I'd just tell him I'm sorry," said Nate.

"What would you need back from George if you said that?" I asked.

"Nothing," replied Nate. "I sure wouldn't want him to have to think about the unfinished stuff between us."

"Maybe you could consider telling him that, Nate. Just telling him that you're sorry and that you don't need anything back from him."

I told Nate that in my experience most of the time "nothing" is not really nothing. It is "something." It is something that has expectations that come along with it. It has unfinished business attached to it. It has an agenda. I think I got *real* nothing from only a couple of people. From the rest I got "something." And whenever I got "something," I felt I had to give something back. A return call. A thank-you note. Some other acknowledgment.

I appreciated the "somethings." Sometimes I even felt I wouldn't have "made it" through some of the hardest moments but for the "somethings." But nothing. That was in a category all by itself. Nothing was blissful. Nothing was soothing. Nothing was a gift that had absolutely no conditions. Nothing was love.

Nate left. I was left alone with the realization that dispensing advice is much easier than living the advice yourself. Nancy, I now admit that I may have had expectations of you. I admit that I may have written these letters to you in anticipation of getting something in return. Not necessarily a letter. But "something."

Nancy, I hereby give you the nothing that I got from Greg. I affirm to you that I'll continue to write to you. You don't have to write back.

Nancy, I love you.

I love you forevermore.

with all my love,

To order additional copies of *Love Letters*

Web: www.itascabooks.com

Phone: 1-800-901-3480

Fax: Copy and fill out the form below with credit card information. Fax to 763-398-0198.

Mail: Copy and fill out the form below. Mail with check or credit card information to:

Syren Book Company
5120 Cedar Lake Road
Minneapolis, MN 55416

Order Form

Copies	Title / Author	Price	Totals
	Love Letters / **Andris A. Baltins**	$16.95	$
	Subtotal		$
	7% sales tax (MN only)		$
	Shipping and handling, first copy		$ 4.00
	Shipping and handling, ___ add'l copies @$1.00 ea.		$
	TOTAL TO REMIT		$

Payment Information:

__ Check Enclosed __ Visa/MasterCard		
Card number:		Expiration date:
Name on card:		
Billing address:		
City:	State:	Zip:
Signature:		Date:

Shipping Information:

__ Same as billing address __ Other (enter below)		
Name:		
Address:		
City:	State:	Zip: